Brain Training

Improving your cognitive functions

Please consult a licensed professional before attempting any techniques outlined in this book.

By reading this document, the reader agrees that under no circumstances is the author responsible for any losses, direct or indirect, which are incurred as a result of the use of information contained within this document, including, but not limited to, — errors, omissions, or inaccuracies.

Table of Contents

Introduction

Research shows that many people struggle with reading, learning, paying attention, and recalling, and chances are you are one of them. A decline in these imperative skills is always a result of weak or declining cognitive abilities.

While brain training is not a new concept, very few people truly know the basics or the various approaches involved in brain training. Thus, brain training is highly recommended for individuals who are keen on improving their cognitive functions.

This is because brain training has the ability of strengthening our cognitive skills since it improves the brain's neural connections. The improvement of neural connections ensures that the brain can process and grasp any incoming information effectively.

The good news is that brain training does so much more. Through a series of mental exercise which have been developed by studying how the brain learns, remembers, thinks, and reads, we are now able to improve our cognitive skills.

In this book, you will learn the basics of brain training. We are also going to look at the science behind brain training and whether brain training truly works. The book also looks at the significant components of an effectual brain training program which means that you will have a clear understanding of what to look for in a brain training program.

You will get to know how to identify a program that works and one that does not work. Brain Training: Improving Your Cognitive Functions also looks at the history of brain training programs and some of the earliest forms of brain training programs.

You will get to know more about the mind-brain relationship and important concepts such as monism and dualism. Finally, you will get to know more about cognitive-based therapies as well as essential CBT tool and techniques and mindfulness.

... faber est suae quisque fortunae ...

Chapter 1
Introduction to Brain Training

Cognitive training/brain training is a technique that's widely employed by neuropsychologists, psychologists, speech therapists, psychiatrists, occupational therapists and numerous clinical rehabilitation professionals as a tool within treatment programs to enhance a person's ability to function properly especially after experiencing neurological disorders like stroke or brain injuries.

These exercises/programs are employed as tools to help attain targeted therapeutic goals like the ability to tolerate frustrations, development of problem-solving strategies, and improvement of self-esteem. Moreover, these programs can also be used within school settings, where they may potentially get rid of problems that are typically associated with learning.

Brain training has the ability to improve the following cognitive functions;

- Attention
- Memory
- reasoning
- Perception
- Judgment
- Planning
- Overall executive functioning
- General learning

There are several research and studies which have shown that developing these cognitive abilities may lead to improvements in emotional stability, self-confidence, and self-awareness.

Furthermore, there are several meta-cognitive training strategies that focus on enhancing positive thinking and coping skills that we can apply interactively when it comes to cognitive training. The primary benefit of cognitive training is that through trying over and over the individual is going to be able to use these new approaches and studies to solve problems that relate to their mental performances.

For instance, a trainer may assist a client in developing cognitive skills required to prioritize or pen down daily tasks. Alternatively, the trainer may help the client improve the skills required to categorize and organize grocery lists or household items by learning how to take a break and take notes quickly during an exercise.

That said, the personal computer is undeniably the most preferred training partner for individuals who are keen on training their minds. One of the main reasons why computer programs are popular is because computer-based training makes it quite easy for trainers to customize their training approaches and also to track progress.

On top of that, it also offers several training exercises, including auditory and visual and also allows the possibility of increasing the difficulty of the task as the client makes progress. The clients will also be directed continually by the program to continue developing their cognitive skills to their maximum potential and capabilities. Moreover, unlike humans, computer programs are not judgmental and thus will never at any given point, lose patience. Finally, people tend to associate computer games with fun and thus this makes it an effective program because it also brings some sense of enjoyment while improving certain cognitive skills.

Do brain training programs work?

Are you feeling like your concentration is slipping away? Do you want to improve your problem-solving skills? Are you interested in preventing several age-related declines in cognitive skills? If you are interested in any of the issues mentioned above, then the brain training industry has something for you.

You have probably have come across such marketing statements online. However, the real question is do brain training computer-based programs work?

Over the years, the brain training industry has grown into a multi-billion-dollar industry. The marketing angle of brain training programs is that by playing various cognitive games may improve multiple cognitive skills that we use in our daily life. In a journal published by Daniel J Simons, a renowned psychologist and his colleagues called many of these claims into question.

Several brain-training programs are based on the concept that practicing several simple cognitive skills within a limited context will improve various cognitive skills in our day to day life.

However, what exactly does science say about brain training games and exercises? Simon and his team looked at the findings of different studies that were published in several peers reviewed journals such as those cited on the blogs and websites of some of the leading brain training companies.

In their analysis, the team found that cognitive training exercises appeared to improve the overall performances on the individuals in the specific trained tasks. Nevertheless, there was minimal data, which proved that cognitive training improves the researcher's performance on tasks that are closely related to the job that they trained on.

On top of that, the researchers found little evidence which proved that cognitive training improves the performance of the participants on tasks that were not related or our day to day cognitive functions. Moreover, the authors also found that there were several studies which suffered from methodological issues, and therefore, many of this did not go hand in hand with the research's best practices.

Therefore, where exactly can we go from here? Simons and his teams offer recommendations for researchers, journalists, funding agencies and the general public. The recommendations postulated by the group will help research centers to analyze their plans for mind-training studies and strengthen their methodologies.

Some of the best practices that the team recommends include the use of sufficient sample size, preregistering studies behind the programs, correction of several comparisons and the acknowledgement of any conflicts of interest by the companies behind brain training programs.

Organizations providing the funding should not only demand the pre-registration of the studies but should also require that these programs employ best practices. Finally, all funding organizations should ensure that the research is transparently and fully reported.

On the other hand, funding organizations must provide adequate funds rigorous large-scale studies required in different areas of research. While doing this, the research organization should weigh the opportunity costs in comparison to other interventions.

Apart from the funding organizations, media houses also have a pivotal role. Journalists and media houses that cover cognitive training research must confirm that the claims made about the studies by brain training companies should match the evidence provided. On top of that, journalists and media outlets should be critical in their coverages to ensure that the public is not in any way misled by the findings from these researches.

Majority of the individuals who are enticed about the claims presented forth by brain training companies are normally the most vulnerable groups. These groups tend to include adults and children who have cognitive deficits, adults who are experiencing a decline in cognitive functions, and finally, people experiencing mental health issues. Policy makers should critically evaluate the claims brought forth by brain-training companies and should also require rigorous standards of research and evidence to ensure that these programs are beneficial to the participants.

Finally, the consumers should weigh carefully the benefits and costs involved when using these brain training exercises. If your main goal is to improve your overall performance on specific trained tasks, then pick a brain training program that will help you achieve that goal. On the other hand, if your goal is to improve a more comprehensive cognitive skill set, then the brain training should be able to help you achieve that. It's essential for the public to be more skeptical about most training programs and thus should examine the quality of the science behind such programs or companies.

Research and studies have shown that people tend to remember information much better when it's encoded. To get the best results, it's essential to ensure that a meaningful connection is made. Elaboration through mnemonic devices, imagery, and the creation of personal links to the material will augment recall.

Testing yourself, instead of just reading important information is a great way to retain memory and long-term learning. Taking space between study sessions instead of cramming everything in one study marathon is also a great way of improving our memory of the information that we are studying.

Studies presented forth by scientists showed that there are several effective methods for enhancing memory. However, many of these methods are still grounded in research. Nonetheless, for many people who are still interested in popular brain training programs, recent studies show that many programs on the market fall short of the effects advertised. Moreover, the research also shows that people may be able to benefit more from the some of the better supported alternatives. \

Does brain training make people smarter?
For quite some time now, brain training is still a hot topic. Despite the controversies surrounding this topic, brain training still continues to be a booming business. Many brain training companies on the market claim that their programs have been designed by scientists as a way of marketing them. However, this does not in any way mean that all brain training programs are bad. We have programs that are not only backed up by scientific studies but are also quite effective.

Years of studies both on humans and animals have shown that the human and animal brain has some plasticity. This is extremely beneficial to people who suffered stroke and are keen on relearning some of the essential cognitive abilities.

However, do we have scientific evidence which shows that brain training can improve a person's overall performance?

An ideal brain training program should be backed up by studies which demonstrate the effects of the respective program rather than the citation of numerous findings and studies.

Some researchers claim that brain/mind training studies which claim to demonstrate noteworthy effects tend to lack wide-ranging applicability. Moreover, these studies have also shown very few exclusive improvements.

On the other hand, there is a group of scientists and researchers who argue that the studies which fail to demonstrate these effects tend to employ approaches that are flawed and apply the recommended methods unsatisfactorily.

No person can dispute the fact that far-reaching training on a specific task will help a person improve on that particular task. However, brain training's acid test is whether extensive training on a task will be able to transfer the acquired abilities to thought processes and other tasks.

In one of the most extensive studies that were ever undertaken, the researchers failed to show a generalization of the training across different tasks.

The researchers performed a six-week study where 11, 430 partakers were taught numerous times each week on several cognitive tasks. The tasks were made to expand memory, reasoning, attention, planning, and visuospatial proficiencies. The developmental effects were specific to each job and failed in transferring to other tasks that the trainees had not been trained on.

Nonetheless, in a recently conducted high-profile study which was performed on older participants, a group of participants employed the use of video games. In this study, the participants were expected to not only drive but also identify certain road signs.

By the end of the study, the older individuals who were 60 to 85 years, ended up becoming more proficient that untrained people who were still in their 20's. The performance levels of the older people were sustained for approximately six months without the need for further training.

That said, what sets this research apart from all the other studies was the fact that the researchers also discovered that the senior adults who participated in the research were able to perform much better in other working memory and attention tests, thereby revealing the transferability of the benefits from a training game to a variety of mental functions.

However, as expected this study has received several criticisms. For instance, some scientists claim that the study was performed on only a small group of participants.

Brain Training and Cognitive Aging

Cognitive aging is one of the effects that comes with aging. Initially, the changes are subtle. However, as time goes by, it will get somewhat difficult to ignore the distractions.

Apart from failing to keep up with the constant chatter of young children, their names may start to slip. Moreover, it will also be memorized while trying to make a phone call. Many of these changes will begin to occur during the late '40s and the '50s. It's essential to point out that they are a normal part of the aging process.

When you go online, you will find several brain training programs which claim to have the ability to help people fight cognitive-drop offs and strengthen their mental muscles. By running around virtual racetracks, recalling patterns, counting the proportions of cooking ingredients the creators of these games claim that the users of these games will be able to enhance their reasoning, problem-solving skills and reasoning.

According to a Michigan University professor who works in the educational psychology and cognitive neuroscience department, Priti Shah, people tend to be aware that their cognitive abilities and skills tend to decline as they grow older. Thus, many of these people are normally more than eager to find new ways which may help to prevent these natural processes. Nonetheless, the big question is, does playing memory games help older adults in their day to day lives?

Will memory games help a person to stay wholly focused while conversing or assist them in remembering whether they had taken their medication or not. Despite all the information that is on the internet, scientists have still not been able to find any conclusive evidence on whether brain training works or not. The FTC fined two business, LearninRX and Luminosity for misleading their customers into believing that the games offered by these two companies could delay or reduce mental deficits that tend to come with aging.

Looking back at history, people have used games such as crosswords and Sudoku to try and improve their cognitive abilities. Renowned figures such as Mark Twain could not overlook the impervious skills of such games. Apart from trying out mental games, Mark Twain went a step further and even came up with his own trivia game, Memory Builder, while working on his book, Adventures of Huckleberry Finn. We look at the detailed history of brain training and mental sports in the next chapter.

However, since then, the brain game industry has experienced tremendous growth. The industry generated a whopping 1 billion dollars in the year 2012. According to projections made by Sharpbrains, this industry is expected to reach 6 billion dollars by the year 2020.

That said, while many of the tasks found within brain training programs are normally based on real neuropsychological tests, many of these tasks seldom translate to more significant real-world tasks. A study which was conducted by 30 scientists in the year 2016 disclosed that brain training exercises helped individuals enhance their performance on the tasks that they trained for. However, the skills that these individuals learned could not be transferred to other tasks that were unrelated, like the overall improvements in processing and memory speed.

Another critical study which was published in the year 2017, pitted regular game against Luminosity's brain training program. The researchers requested one group of the participants to play commercial video games, while the remaining group to play Luminosity games for five-time every week for a maximum of 10 weeks. By the end of the training session, the participants who were in both groups showed almost the same improvements when it comes to standardized cognitive measures. However, the same results were displayed by a separate control group that did not participate in the experiment.

According to Shah, the participants showed improvements mainly because they took part in cognitive tests. Nonetheless, the results from the study suggested that the games offered by Luminosity could not enhance real-life cognitive abilities. With that said, this does not in any way mean that brain training lacks potential. Just because a specific program does not help with a sure thing does not mean that a different intellectually stimulating experience or cognitive ability it's not going to improve the outcomes for a specific group of people.

Indeed, there are several studies which suggest that brain training games might offer limited benefits to people who are in the early phases of Alzheimer's disease.

A report based on the ACTIVE study revealed that training to enhance the processing speeds reduced the chances of older adults developing dementia, ten years down the line. The participants who were involved in the exercise which entailed the identification of images that flashed across the screen quickly we're able to reduce their risks of developing dementia by more than 29 percent.

On the other hand, participants who were part of brain training which involved improvement of reasoning skills and memory boosts experienced an insignificant reduction in the risk to contract dementia.

According to Katz, there exists no silver bullet. People who are keen on preserving their cognitive abilities must try and incorporate various things into their day to day routines. If you are training for a big athletic event or preparing for a marathon, then your focus should not only be on running. You should also focus on other things such as cross-training, sleep schedule, dieting, and several other things that will play a key role in your overall performance.

Scientists and researchers have already begun looking at the role of multidimensional approaches in supporting a healthier brain. There is some evidence which suggests that physical exercises play a crucial role when it comes to maintaining mental skills, improving the quality of our sleep, and reducing stress.

Exercises also help us with various social activities such as playing cards with our friends, dancing or knitting. According to Katz, the majority of this is still correlation in nature. However, it still provides concepts and ideas for several things that we may explore in the future, which might prove cognition.

Components of an effective brain training program

There are several activities which make brain training quite effective. Any great brain training program or exercise must incorporate all of these components. The components that you should look out for in a brain training program include;

Personalization

A good training program must first assess your performance so that you can be able to receive personalized and unique training. Different studies and research show that during the initial stages, it's important to ensure that the trainee is challenged but not overwhelmed. The trainee can only achieve their best when they work at optimum levels.

Goal specific

The brain exercises or activity offered must be designed to target the specific brain functions required in our day to day lives. Therefore, the service provider must offer exercises which meet these specific goals.

Motivating

As it is the case with everything in life, practice always makes it perfect. The more a person trains, the better they end up becoming. Therefore, we highly recommend daily training sessions with brain exercises and games for around 15 minutes. You can always try getting your family and friends to join you during your practice sessions. Having people to train with you will make the entire process extremely motivating. Regardless of age, you will definitely find brain training quite enjoyable. Thus anyone can join.

Challenging

Studies show that when a task does not increase in its level of difficulty, then the brain will end up becoming bored and thereby begin to automate the entire process. Therefore, after some time, you are not going to be challenged anymore. When you play a game such as Sudoku, once you get better, your brain is never going to feel challenged. This is due to the fact that the brain tends to restructure itself, and therefore it's going to master and automate the challenge.

While this is great for certain tasks especially those that we have to do on a day to day basis, like riding a bike or driving a car, the human brain requires a new set of challenges to stay fit. With each process, the level of the brain exercises should increase, thereby keeping the brain challenged on all occasions and working at an optimum level.

Picking Brain Training Programs

Scientists have touted brain training programs as one of the ways of preventing cognitive decline due to aging. There are a number of products on the market that are available for purchase. However, the issue remains are these products really effective. We have looked at the benefits of peer-reviewed intervention studies which have looked at commercial computerized training products in people above 50 years, who are healthy.

In the study, 7 programs were identified whose claims for efficacy have been supported by evidence. Out of all the seven programs, only two of the programs were able to meet the highest standards — these Cognifit and BrainHQ. The exercises offered by BrainHQ adjusted the difficulty on a constant basis determined by the participant's performance. One set of the exercises, including the matching of a pair of syllables, identifying details in a verbally presented narrative and reconstructing the sequences of instructions that were given verbally.

The other types of exercises are engaging visually. For instance, an exercise asks the user to assume that he/she is a horticulturist. To grow plants, the users are asked to match photos one after the other, a few moments after they emerge on the screen. On the other hand, the exercises from Cognifit LTD contain at least 20 different tasks. In one of these tasks offered by Cognifit, the user is asked to remember a path that a hot air balloon takes and reproduce the exact route.

In a different assignment, a letter grid will appear at the center of your screen. A photo of a popular object will appear on the screen's left corner. In this task, you will be asked to discover the name of the object on the letter grid. All in all, both of these programs offer reasonable clinal evidence to show that they are effective when it comes to clinical aging.

As discussed above, only 40 percent of the programs offered to come with evidence.

Thus, to establish whether a specific brain training exercise is effectual, it's significant to carefully look at the scientific substantiation behind the program or exercise, as well as the purpose for which the program is recommended. For instance, to encourage healthy-brain aging or reduce the effects of dementia and other types of neurological diseases, it's important to understand the precise principle that's behind the overall design for these types of exercises.

For this study, 18 computerized cognitive training programs that were accessible across the world were selected. All these brain training programs claimed to have some sort of scientific evidence behind them,

Of all these programs, only seven programs were actually assessed by scientific/peer-reviewed studies which reported proper outcome measures of these programs on precise brain-related domains like reasoning, process speed, reasoning, executive functions, and memory. The study settled for studies which had been done on healthy adults that were 50 years and above of age.

The specific trials were considered as well-made only if the designs were randomized clinical tests that had a control group. The studies were then classified as being moderate, poor, or high quality on a checklist that ran from one to ten. Trials which scored anything greater than six, was considered to be of high quality. On the other hand, trials which had scores of five and six were considered to be of moderate quality. Finally, trials which had a score of less than five were considered to be of poor quality.

The next step was classifying seven brain training programs that were computer-based into three main categories according to the strength of the evidence which supported the program's claims of efficacy. The process entailed the examination of the quality and quantity of the clinical trials that were applied on each occasion.

The researchers classified all the 7-computerized brain programs into three major categories. The categories created were based on the evidence's strength which supports the efficacy claims. The process entailed an exhaustive examination of the superiority and the magnitude of the clinical tests that were applied to every illustration.

Level One

The programs under this classification had on the very least, two well-made controlled trials. One of these programs was of very high standards and quality. Two of all the brain training program were able to meet this criterion. (Cognifit and BrainHQ)

Level Two

The programs under this classification were supported by one controlled test that was randomized. The controlled trial was of high quality. All of the programs that were assessed; only three programs were classified under this level. (BrainAge2, My Brain Trainer and Cogmed).

Level Three

The programs under this category were only supported by one controlled trial that was of either poor or moderate design. Of all the seven programs, only two fell under this category; Luminosity and Dakim.

The findings of the study indicated that some of the computerized cognitive training programs were backed by some evidence which claimed to play a key role in the promotion of healthy brain aging. Nonetheless, these types of programs should be validated further by making use of brain imaging methods to look at their action mechanism.

Picking an Effectual Program

Cognitive training programs tend to feature a number of exercises which specifically target specified cognitive domains like reasoning, executive functions, memory, and processing speed. The most effective exercises tent to be devised on the proposition on the human brain's ability to reconnect and rewire, also known as the neuroplasticity principle. These types of computerized exercises tend to be adaptive according to the individual's capability. Moreover, they are also continuously challenging and can either be visual/and or audio interactive.

Some of the features that you should look out for in a brain training program before choosing include;

- Whether the program can be tailored to address your needs such as brain ageing, learning, concentration and brain ageing.
- Whether the program has been validated scientifically
- Whether the program is engaging and adaptive
- Whether the program is unremittingly challenging
- Whether the program qualities are visually and/or audio interactive
- Whether the program offers feedback about any progress that you make.

Programs which train the human brain to become entirely responsive when using certain tasks and to increase the difficulty levels are believed to have the ability to rewire our neural pathways according to the principle of neuroplasticity.
How to identify a program that may not work

In the study's review process, more than 18 training programs were identified. Out of these programs, 11 of them had not to sort of empirical evidence or clinical trials to show that these programs were effective when it came to the promotion of healthy/accepted brain-aging.

Programs which train the human brain to become more responsive are believed to assist the rewiring of the neural pathways. One way that you can use to identify programs which lack adequate evidence includes going to the website of the program and establish whether that company offers specific links to specified studies that are relevant to your purpose.

Majority of these websites only provide evidence that is supportive. These means that many of these websites do not in any way refer to specified clinical-trials but rather will quote certain principles such as the ability of the human's brain to rewire and also site programs which are used in other programs. Very few websites have managed to lists studies which measure the effect of the program that's in question.

The findings from research and studies which were double-bonded (whether both the user and investigator do not know whether the intervention is a placebo or real) randomized and featured control groups which meet high standards of clinical-trials tend to be more reliable in comparison to the non-randomized trials which did not have any control conditions.

Training programs for the prevention of cognitive decline

Nonetheless, evidence with regards how or where some of these software programs have an effect on the plasticity of the brain cells or whether the connection within the human brain is somewhat lacking. Assessments which make use of specified biological markers of the Alzheimer's diseases like brain and blood imaging would improve the clinical validation of various cognitive training programs.

Assessments that make use of specified Alzheimer's disease or neurodegenerative disorders biological markers such as brain and blood imaging were going to improve clinical validation of these applications substantially. This was going to enable a greater understanding of the connections to present between human cognition and brain training applications. It will also provide great insights into novel therapeutic pathways.

There is a possibility that computerized exercises which are constantly thought-provoking and quite malleable can help to rewire any lost connections which are associated with dementia, in an individual's later years. However, presently, the evidence and research present has failed to fully confirm the applications ability to avert the onset of dementia. Therefore, more in-depth studies and follows are needed.

Irrespective as to whether newfangled neural-pathways are found, there are some psychological exercises that might work just by enhancing blood circulation to the brain, in the same way, mental exercises work. Therefore, it's possible to achieve healthy brain aging through the improvement and maintenance of cognitive functions through avenues like brain training as well as social interactions, diets, exercises, and other crucial life strategies.

What you should know about brain training programs

While everyone wants to be smarter, each person has their own reasons for wanting to improve their cognitive functions. There are those who tend to worry above age-related cognitive decline, while there are others who are keen on improving their performance at work. There are those people who want to be faster when it comes to solving those irksome sudoku puzzles.

As discussed earlier in the chapters, there are a number of choices in the market that consumers can choose from to increase their cognitive functions. Cogfit, Elevate, and Luminosity are some of the few companies that are widely known for their brain training programs. Most of the programs are available at modest cost and are available in a number of platforms including mobile devices. Since everyone loves games, the commitment mind seems minor.

Nonetheless, what exactly do we know about these games? The science behind the games may be daunting, especially if the company decides to share scientific research.

While there is no person who will be able to tell you, what program is going to work for your personal needs, there are three crucial things that you need to know about these brain training programs. These three things will help you to fully understand the principles that are behind these games and also why there are some instances when they work and other instances they do not work.

The training should be adaptive

To understand this concept, let is begging with a simple yet understandable analogy; darts. If you were keen on becoming an experienced dart player, how exactly would you start? It goes without saying that you are not going to stand about 20 yards away from a dashboard and then start throwing the darts. Instead, you are going to begin taking a few shorts with moderate success standing a few meters from the dashboard. Depending on your performance, you will either move forward or backward. In simple terms, you are going to adapt.

This concept is also applicable to brain training. While beginning your brain training program, it's not advisable to begin the brain training program by trying to master a 50—item list. The aim is to begin slowly and then expand slowly. While expanding, it's extremely important always to remember our limits. When using brain training as a brain training alternative, it's important always to attempt what's just beneath our reach.

While this may sound quite simple, it also means that training that's easy is not going to offer any benefits. Thus, you should ensure that you avoid any brain training program that is not adaptive and also games which do not severely challenge your brain. The constant need for a challenge is the main reason why there is very little scientific support for cognitive training within the academic realm. Spending 30 hours memorizing lists is not going to improve our brain unless the lists are different for each person and are of the proper length. This, in turn, makes it quite hard to find your training sweet spot.

The training should be varied

Memory is a mystery that many scientists are still trying to understand. For instance, we have a visual memory and verbal memory. Each of these forms of memory exercises different parts of the human brain. Many great brain training programs will involve a well-designed sensory experience of sounds and sights to enhance these sperate memories and perpetual systems. The great ones are going to tap different verbal retention and math abilities.

It's important to point out that intelligence does not involve a single skill, and thus, training or working on one thing does not necessarily promise benefits in other places. Always keep in mind that to experience the benefits of brain training in a broad sense, then you will have to train up in a variety of skills. Training in a variety of skills has numerous benefits, including the fact that it prevents you from getting bored or tired from training on just a single task. If you focus on building skill, then you expect the real benefits to taking some time.

The training should be generalized

When you take upon brain training programs, it's important to point out that you are not just trying to grasp the skills that you will be training on. As a matter of fact, many of these games are totally different from anything that you are going to experience in real life. The hope of brain training programs or games is that the practice that you will receive is applicable to real-world abilities.

While this is the initial concept behind many of these games, a bigger percentage of the skills that you will get from brain training programs do not always generalize. While there are studies that have showed small improvements in the participants IQ and other things after brain training, many studies have shown that commercial brain training programs offer no real value. As a matter of fact, many scientists have warned consumers to stay away from brain training programs that are sold online.

Many at times, these programs will feel productive mainly because the participant will get better and better in time. However, this does not necessarily mean that they are making the participant smarter in any way. This might lead to a misleading advertisement. Any company that claims to have programs which claim 200 percent improvements should be able to answer the question, improvement on what? Majority of companies offering braining training programs tend to avoid this question by citing research and studies on brain plasticity, a meaningless term which points out that our brain is constantly changing. It's obvious that our brain changes. A brain which does not change is technically a brick and not a brain.

How exactly could you be able to remember what you had for breakfast? Every social interaction or memory alters the brain, and this is beyond any doubt. Nonetheless, the real question is whether these changes entail some universal abilities to solve problems. Unless a brain training program makes specific promises with regards on how the company's brain training program generalizes, then it's important to stay away from these games. While you can always go and sign up for Cogfit and Luminosity or any other program that offers to increase your cognitive functions, the choice is always up to.

Chapter 2

History of Brain Training

The popularity of brain training programs continues to rise as the day goes by. Brain training programs continue to be a part of the ever-growing digital industry which generated more than 1 billion dollars in revenue in the year 2012. While this is the case, the level and extent to which these games improve brain functioning continue to be a hotly debated topic. Nonetheless, there is still an agreement that brain training as a new commercial phenomenon is still fresh.

Established in the year 2001, Cogfit is undeniably one of the earliest brain training companies. Other brain training companies include Posit Science which was founded in the year 2003 and Brain Age which was released in the year 2005, for the gaming device, Nintendo DS.

Take a look at this marketing line "Build the mind just like the way a physical instructor builds muscles". You may think that this line is borrowed from the marketing ads for one of these modern companies. However, the line is taken from a 100-year-old mind training product advertisement that was used by a group of more than 500,000. The group that used this product include the British Prime Minister at the time.

Nonetheless, unlike mnemonic systems which came before this device, the program was known as Pelmanism and was focused on similar mental functions such as creativity, concentration, and attention. Tasks that are still targeted by all new brain training programs. The previous systems for memory training were prevalent in the 19th century. These mnemonic systems like Memory Builder that was built by Mark Twain involved many strategies and tricks which allowed people to recall facts much better like dates and names.

On the other hand, Pelmanism eventually evolved from similar mnemonic systems developed during the 20th century in London into something that looked much similar to new brain training.

The Pelman Scientific Training Program appeared in periodicals such as Popular Mechanics and The Strand. The members also are known as Pelmanists were each mailed with a variety of booklets which had titles like Knowledge and the Senses, Concentration and Principles of Mental Connection. Each of this booklet began by explaining the topic which reflects a selection of contemporary pop psychology of the time like the views of William James on creating auto-suggestions and habits, which was a new self-hypnosis technique of the 20th century. After completing the short readings, the participants were expected to fill out the exercise sheets and then mail them back to the Pelman Institute for review.

Chapter 3

Brain training Exercises and Games

More and more people are beginning to realize that the human brain needs to receive regular exercise and be taken care of, just like all the other parts of the physical structure. The human mind has been designed to automate processes when possible. Thus, the brain loves to create routines now and then so that it can either automate complex tasks and conserve energy. However, the only challenge is that once the brain does this, it provides the human brain with very little stimulation. This is why majority of the highly recommended brain training exercises, also known as neurotics, are all based on forcing the human brain to break free from its daily routines.

Moreover, doing things such as giving the brain new and exciting experience which combine our physical senses such as touch, hearing, taste, vision and smell together with emotional insights are going to help in the simulation of more connections between the various brain regions, thereby making the surrounding cells much stronger and more resistant to the expected effects which come with ageing.

As mentioned in the first chapter, we now have games which exercise the brain so that we can be able to trick the mind while having fun and keeping ourselves mentally fit. New strategies and tricks which help to keep the human brain much younger are being created each day.

However, for the moment, here is a comprehensive list for some of our highly recommended methods that will help you start out with mental routines, thereby making them a part of your day to day mental fitness practices. However, you should ensure that you prevent yourself from getting extremely good at these routines. Once these routines become a part of your daily life, they will no longer be challenging for your brain.

Ten mental exercises that truly work

Apart from regular exercises, there are other ways that you can always give your brain its mental workout routine without having to empty your wallet. While brain training software is everywhere, the studies and research that we discussed in-depth have shown that these games are yet to show any noticeable neurological benefits, especially in older adults.

In review that was published in the year 2014 in the peer-reviewed website, PLOS Medicine, a team of Australian researchers examined 52 different research and studies on on-screen cognitive training which was conducted on 4,8885 participants. The study found that these games are not active when it came to improving a person's overall brain performance.

Experts highly recommend sticking to cognitive training which involves real-world activities. The exercises or activities to strengthen cognitive function should be able to offer challenge and novelty. According to David Eagleman, an assistant professor and neuroscientist, any silly suggestion can work. While driving home, you can opt to pick a different route. Alternatively, you can also decide to brush your teeth using your less dominant hand because the human brain tends to work through association, which explains why it's much easier to memorize a song while listening to the song regularly that it's to remember similar words without any music playing on the background. Thus, the more we involve our senses, the easier it is going to be easy to remember.

A great place to start with your cognitive training is the newspaper. You can begin the process by playing simple games such as word games and sudoku. You can also head over to the pages with comic strips where you are going to find pictures that are different from the other. This is according to John E. Morley, a director of the world-renowned Louis University and a bestselling author. Apart from word games Dr. John E. Morley also recommends some of the following exercises to help us to sharpen our cognitive skills.

1.   Testing your recall-For this ability, you can create a list, probably a grocery list, to-do lists and anything which might come to your mind and then memorize the list. After an hour or later, you can then test yourself to see how many items you will be able to recall. You can make the entries on your list as thought-

provoking as you can to ensure the highest levels of mental stimulation.

2. Play Music-You can teach yourself how to play a new musical instrument that you have never played before, or join a choir. Studies indicate that learning something that's not only new and complex over long periods is highly beneficial to the aging mind.

3. Do math using your head-You should try and figure out math problems in your head without using a pen, paper, computer or pencil. You can decide to increase the difficulty of the problem by ensuring that you walk at the same time while doing the calculations.

4. Take up, cooking classes. You should teach yourself how to cook new cuisines. Because cooking makes uses of a number of sensors such as touch, taste, feeling, smell, and sight which uses different parts of the brain, cooking is an excellent alternative for cognitive training.

5. Learning foreign languages. The hearing and listening involved while learning a foreign language tend to stimulate the human brain. A wide vocabulary range has been linked with a reduction in cognitive decline.

6. Create word pictures. You should try and visualize the right spelling of a given the word in your head and then try and

contemplate on other words which either begin or end with similar letters.

7. Draw a map. Upon returning to your home from work or after visiting a new place, you can try and create a representation of the given area. Try and repeat this drill every time you pay a visit to a new location.

8. Dare your taste buds. While eating, you should try and identify the respective ingredients in your meals, such as the subtle spices and herbs.

9. Refine your eye-hand abilities. You should take a new hobby which involves the use of fine-motor skills such as drawing, knitting, assembling a puzzle or knitting.

10. Learn new games or sports. Begin by doing a rather simple athletic exercise which utilizes both the body and mind such as tennis, golf, or yoga.

It is not going to take long before people realize that they can be able to take several steps to ensure that their brains are healthy, the same way people know and understand that they can be able to prevent or stop heart diseases. In the years that will come, the chances are that brain wellness is going to be at the same level as cardiovascular health because it has already been established that leading a healthy brain life works miracles.

Impact of brain training exercises and games

Therefore, what are some of the impacts of brain training exercises? Several research established that participants who received brain training which involved cognitive abilities had improvements in their day to day lives which included cognitive skills. The memory improvements eventually translated into real-life activities like recalling when you are required to take medications and which are some of the items that a person needed to get from the local grocery store. On the other hand, speed-response training related to things such as the reaction time that a person had while driving.

However, the question is, did the effect of this training truly last? Five years down the line after the completion of the training exercise, the participants from a total of three groups displayed the critical improvements in the areas that they had received cognitive training for. Nonetheless, the effect eventually declined for those people who were in the memory groups. After a total of 10 years, the memory group stopped displaying the improvements while other groups, including those in the speed-processing groups, did.

These results eventually revealed that after a total of 10 years, more than 74 percent of the people who had received reasoning training were still able to show significant improvements on top of baseline levels. On the other hand, individuals who were in the processing speed groups showed approximately 62 percent improvements on top of the baseline levels. Finally, the people who were within the memory group showed no improvement at all.

The authors of this study suggest that the findings from this research were hopefully going to encourage other scientists and researchers to further look at how these processes genuinely work and also come up with effective training programs for cognitive skills. The researchers also suggest that if we were able to introduce interventions which could delay the commencement of functional impairment by at least 6 years, then the number of persons who were going to be affected by the year 2050 will reduce by more than 38 percent, which will be of great value and significance to the public health. Putting the large population of old aged people into consideration, these types of improvements are going to have a crucial impact on the functioning and mental health of the older generation.

Processing speeds are highly encouraging, according to Jonathan W. King, who was the co-author of this study and the cognitive aging programming director at the National Health Institute. According to King, these self-reported improvements in our day to day lives are quite impressive. However, we do not as of yet honestly know whether they are going to allow the older people to live on their own much longer. If these self-reported improvements truly worked, then even the smallest effect was going to be extremely important for adults, family members, and care providers.

Do these exercises work?

The promise that brain-changing games offer is quite hard to resist. Everyone would like to improve their thinking and memory while having fun, especially when we grow older and begin to experience the effects of aging on our cognitive functions. This is what exactly products such Luminosity promises to offer. These computer-based training programs claim that they can improve our cognitive services and so much more. These set of games target attention and memory. Moreover, as we continue to play them, they tend to get more complicated.

Chapter 4

Mind Body Relationship

Mind-Body Problems

The mind-body problem is a scientific approach that's concerned to the extent in which the body and mind are either the same or separate entities. The mind is all about consciousness, mental processes, and thoughts. On the other hand, the body is all about the structure of the mind/brain and the physical aspects of brain-neurons. However, while this is the case, there has been a question that many scientists and psychologist have always tried to answer. Is the human mind part of the body or the is the human body a segment of the mind? If these two are dissimilar, then how exactly do they interrelate with each other? Moreover, which of the two is in charge of the other?

There have been lots of theories that have been devised to try and explain the correlation between what we call the mind (conscious thinking that experiences our thoughts) and the brain which is part of the human body.

What is Dualism

In Metaphysics, dualism refers to the belief that there are two different kinds of reality, immaterial (spiritual) and material (physical). In mind, philosophy, dualism refers to the position that the body and mind are in some way different or separate from one another and that mental phenomenon are non-physical in some respects.

We can contrast dualism with different types monism including (idealism and Physicalism) and also with pluralism (holds that there are different types of substances rather than two). Dualism appeals to common sense intuition of many people who are non-physically trained people. The physical and mental to most people appear to have different and conflicting properties. Mental events tend to have a certain subjective quality, also known as qualia or the way things seem to us while physical activities tend not to possess this quality.

Scientists and researchers who criticize dualism have brought forth the argument that how can something that's immaterial affect something that's material (problem/issue of causal interaction).

With the knowledge that's gotten from modern science, very few neuroscientists may consider supporting dualism. On the other hand, monistic beliefs such as Physicalism are now widespread within philosophy.

The history of dualism

We can trace the concept of duality back to Aristotle and Plato as well as the early Yoga and Sankhya schools which taught Hindu philosophy. Plato came up with the now popular Theory of Forms. The Theory of Forms interjected that the immaterial and distinct substances of objects that we perceive are nothing but mere shadows. Plato argued that for the intellect to access these universal ideas and concepts, the minds must first become an immaterial and non-physical entity.

Aristotle, on the other hand, brought forth the argument that if intellect were a specified material organ or a part of a real organ, then intelligence would be limited to receiving specified types of information (in the same manner that our eyes are restricted to accepting visual data. Since intellect has the ability to receive and reflect on different types of data, then it's not a physical organ, thereby confirming that it's immaterial.

Early in the days, Neo-Platonic Christians acknowledged Plato's theory of forms. With this group, the soul was a substance of every human being. On the other hand, the body was copy or shadow of these form of eternal wonders. According to St. Thomas Aquinas, the human soul was a substance of the human being, however, just like Aristotle's ideology it was only through the soul's manifestation within the human body that a person could be identified as a being.

Nonetheless, dualism was expounded and studied further in the 17th century by Rene Descartes. Descartes was the first person to come up with the mind-body problem in the manner in which the concepts exists today. Moreover, Descartes was also the first person to identify the human mind with self-awareness and consciousness. He also distinguished the soul from the brain, which he considered to be the physical home of intelligence.

Descartes realized that while he could doubt whether he has a body or not (it might be because it's an illusion or he was dreaming) he could not doubt that he had a mind, which gave him the suggestion that the mind and body are different entities. Nonetheless, the material and immaterial mind (ontologically distinct substances) interact casually in an unspecified way through the body's pineal gland.

Types of dualism

Substance dualism, also known as cartesian dualism claims that the mind is a substance that exists independently-The material itself cannot think while the mental does cover any physical space. This form of dualism was defended famously by Descartes. It's compatible with many theologies that claim immortal souls exists in an independent existence real which is distinct from the physical world.

Property Dualism: Also referred to as Token Dualism, Property Dualism upholds that the mind is among a group of properties which emerge from the human brain. While this is the case, the mind is not a separate substance. Therefore, when matter is arranged in an appropriate way, i.e., like the way we organize human bodies, then mental properties will emerge.

The three forms of property dualism include;

Interactionism-Allows that mental causes like desires and beliefs can produce material effects. Descartes was for the idea that this type of interaction always occurs in a person's pineal gland.

Occasionalism- Occasionalism is a type of Dualism which asserts that a physical basis of interaction between the immaterial and the material is impossible. On the other hand, the interactions that occur are caused by God's intervention on every occasion. The primary proponent of occasionalism was Nicholas Malebranche.

Parallelism-A type of occasionalism holds that mental causes result in only psychological effects, while physical objects tend to lead to physical impacts. However, God has created a harmony that's pre-established such that it appears as if the mental and physical events are caused or will cause one another. This rather unusual view was advocated notably by Gottfried Leibniz.

Epiphenomenalism: This approach holds that mental events are causally inert. This means that they do not have physical consequences. Physical activities have the ability to cause other physical events, while physical phenomena have the capability of producing mental events. However, mental events might not cause anything mainly because they are causally inert by-products of the physical activities that occur within the human brain. This type of doctrine was formulated during the 19th century by non-=other than Thomas Hobbes.

Predicate Dualism-This concept argues that several predicates s required to make sense of this world and that every physiological experience that people go through cannot be described in the physical predicates of the natural languages.

Epistemological Dualism-It's also referred to as Indirect Realism or Representations. Epistemological Dualism is a view that the world that we see in pure conscious experience is merely a miniature virtual-reality model of the world within an internal representation.

Monism

Monism refers to the theological and metaphysical view that the body and mind are one, and that there exist no fundamental divisions since a cohesive set of laws underlie everything. At the deepest analysis level, the universe is either one thin or made of one primary type of stuff. Monism is the opposite of dualism, which holds that are exist two types of substances and from pluralism which advocates that there are different types of materials.

Monism is based on monad's concept, which is derived from monos, a Greek term that means without division or single. Several Pre-Socratic philosophers termed reality as monistic and came up with many explanations for this reality. (Unchanging, undivided, unmoving sphere, one, Thales, Anaximenes, Anaximander, and Heraclitus.

The concept of monism is widely used in several contexts within ethics, philosophy of mind, epistemology, and ethics; however, the underlying idea is that of oneness. While dualism tends to distinguish the body and soul, spirit and matter, subject and object, force and matter, monism refute that such a distinction occurs or merges the two in a higher unity.

With that said, the term monism is relatively recent, as it was first used during the 19th century by Christian Von Wolff, a German philosopher. It was used to differentiate the different forms of philosophical thoughts which attempted to eliminate the dichotomy of the mind and body.

Types of Monism

Monism can be divided into three basic or more classes.

Idealistic monism

Also referred to mentalistic monism,

This doctrine fashions the concept that the mind is everything that exists. That is that the only existing element is mental, and the external world is either an illusion which is created by our minds or mental itself. Therefore, there in only but one reality, eternal and immutable, which some people, including Hindu philosophers of ancient terms, have termed God the idealistic spiritual monism. On the other hand, philosophers who came before the Socratic era were content with the label "the one" or being. This kind of idealistic monism continued to recur through history from Gottfried Leibniz to Neoplatonists to the likes of George Berkeley, to G.W.F Hegel and German Idealism.

Materialistic Monist: This doctrine advocates that there is one reality matter. The reality matter can be a group of atoms, world-building substances, or cosmic nebula. This doctrine also holds that it's only the physical which is real and that the mental element can be reduced into the physical part. People who supported this doctrine include Bertrand Russell and Thomas Hobbes. In the 20th century, this was the dominant doctrine.

With materialistic doctrine there are two primary forms;

Reductive physicalism: This doctrine asserts that all mental properties and states will ultimately be explained by the scientific accounts of the physiological states and processes. It has been the most popular form of materialist doctrine of the 20th century. We have two main types of physicalism;

Reductive Physicalism: Reductive physicalism asserts that all mental properties and states are going to be eventually expounded by scientific accounts of physiological states and process. During the 20th century, it was the most popular form. With reductive physicalism there are three main types;

Behaviorism: It holds that mental states are descriptions of behaviors that we observe.

Type identity Theory: Type identity theory advocates that specified mental states are similar to specified internal and physical states of the human brain.

Functionalism: Functionalism holds we can characterize mental states in non-mental functional properties terms.

Non-reductive physicalism: Non-reductive physicalism argues while the brain is everything that there is to the human mind, the vocabularies and predicates that are used in rational explanations and descriptions cannot be reduced to the lower levels and language of physical science. Therefore, mental states will depend on physical states. Therefore, there cannot be any change within the mind without some changes in the physical world.

When it comes to non-reductive physicalism, there are three main types. They include;

Anomalous monism: Anomalous monism states that mental events tend to be identical with the real events. However, the psychic is anomalous. What are these mental events are not only entirely real but also similar to physical matter? However, they are not regulated by stringent physical laws. Thus, all psychological elements or things are physical; however not all material things are mental. Donald Davidson first proposed these doctrines during the 1970s.

Emergentism: Emergentism is a doctrine that entails a layered view of nature with all the layers arranged in increasing complexity with each layer corresponding to its unique science. Eliminativism is a type of emergentism which holds that individuals innate understanding of the human mind is flawed and is going to be ultimately replaced by an alternative (neuroscience).

Neutral Monism: A dual-aspect theory, neutral monism maintains existence entails one of type of primal substance that is neither physical or mental. However, the content has the capability of physical or psychological aspects/attributes. Therefore, there exist some other neutral substances, initially labeled as nature or essence or God, and that both the mind-matter are all properties of this unknown substance. Bertrand Russell and Baruch Spinoza adopted this position.

Reflexive monism: It's a dual aspect theory which argues that the necessary stuff that makes up the universe has the capabilities of manifesting both in a conscious and physical experience like human beings which may then have a view of themselves or the world. This is a contemporary take on a concept that has been present within the rational thought for hundreds of years. Some of the evidence includes Vedic writings such as the Upanishads and beliefs from ancient Egypt.

Nonetheless, there are instances when a different analysis is used:

Substantial monism: Under this view, there is one substance, and all diversity is ultimately unreal. This is a view that was advocated for by the likes of Spinoza.

Attribute monism: Refers to the view which there is only one kind of thing. However, there are lots of individual elements under this category, and therefore, the reality is finally composed of lots of things instead of one. Idealistic monism and materialistic monism are thus different types of attributive monism.

Absolute monism: A view which holds that there exists only one substance and thus only one being, as it is the case with Advaita Vedanta, an ancient Hindu philosophy.

Mind-Body Debate

Psychology has numerous approaches with many taking juxtaposing outlooks on whether the human body and mind are related or separate entities. Thinking is considered to be a mental event. However, it can cause behavior or movement to occur (for example, muscles move as a result of thoughts). Thinking can thus be said that it makes things happen. i.e., the mind affects matter.

Behaviorists are for the concept that we should restrict psychology to observable actions such as stimulus and response. Moreover, behaviorists believe that our thought process like the mind cannot be examined objectively and technically and thus should be overlooked. On the other hand, there is some radical behaviorist who believes that the human mind is not present.

Biologists who champion that the mind does not exist because there exists no form of physical structure constituting the mind agree with this approach. However, biologists on the other hand argue that the brain is going to be ultimately discovered to be the human mind. The human brain, together with its cells, structures, and neural connections, is going along with scientific research aimed at ultimately discern the mind.

Behaviorists and biologists who believe that a single type of reality exists, the one that we may touch, see or feel then are referred to as monists. As mentioned earlier monism refers to the belief/idea that the brain and the human mind are one.

Nonetheless, behaviorists and biologists are not able to account for the phenomenon known as hypnosis. Orne and Hilgard at one point in time, looked at this in-depth. The two scientists placed the participants in a hypotonic stupor. Through hypnotic trance, the two scientists told the participants that they were going to be touched using a piece of metal that was red hot. However, instead of being affected with scorching metal, the participants were pocked using a pencil.

All the hypnotized partakers developed a skin outbreak in the form of water blisters. The reaction was as if they were touched using hot metal. That said, this is an excellent example of mind-controlling the response of the body. The same results have been achieved on patients who were placed under hypnosis to control pain.

This, in turn, contradicts the monism proposition, since the human body is not expected to react to any unconscious suggest in any manner. This specific study supports the concept of dualism, which points out that our physical form and mind function independently.

In similar fashion humanists such as Carl Rogers were to go ahead and dispute materialist monism. The humanists are for the belief that subjective experiences happen to be the only way that we can analyze human conduct. Humanists do not deny the fact that the material world exists. However, they are for the belief that every person's soul and independent approach to the defining reality which is essential.

Within the field of mental illnesses, people with schizophrenia may not describe their deeds as sickly, but instead, they will believe that they had a discernment into a manifestation that no other person experiences. This is the main reason why humanists are for the belief that the study of how we view ourselves is significant.

Nonetheless, the issue of the correlation between reality and consciousness from an idiosyncratic view has problems. An insecure schizophrenia who tends to believe that postal servicemen are government proxies sent to kill humans is psychologically ill. They may require medical care even if they do not pose a danger to the public or themselves.

Recently released research from several cognitive psychologists have stressed the benefits of this particular debate. The psychologists have taken artificial intelligence's computer correlation and then applied the analogy to the discussion. These group of people argues that we can compare the human brain to computer hardware which is wired or connected to the body. Thus, the human mind can be compared to software, as it allows several software applications to run.

We can account this to the distinctive reactions that people tend to have when exposed to similar stimulus. This concept ties closely with cognitive mediational practices. When it comes to computer analogies, we have been presented with a new dualism version that allows people to incorporate contemporary terms such as software and rather than Descartes philosophical proposition.

Chapter 5

Cognitive Brain Therapy

Irrespective as to whether you are familiar with psychology or not, chances that you have already come across the term cognitive behavioral therapy. CBT is a famous talk therapy technique that's practiced throughout the world.

If you have had a session with a psychiatrist, mental health therapist, or counselor within a professional setting, the chances are that you have already been a part of CBT. If you have already heard your family members of friends talk about how psychological/mental health professionals assisted them in identifying useless patterns and thoughts and then changing them to work more effectively towards specific ideas, then you have already heard of CBT's impact.

As a widely employed tool in a psychologist's toolbox, CBT is based on fundamental principles that ensure CBT will have positive outcomes when implemented.

In this chapter, we are going to look CBT in-depth and also how you can apply CBT's ideologies to enhance your life and your clients'.

What is CBT?

CBT is a form of therapy that aims at changing our patterns and thoughts, our unconscious and conscious beliefs, our behavior and our attitude to assist us in facing certain difficulties and being able to achieve specific goals. The first psychologists to practice CBT is Aaron Beck. Just like many mental health experts, Beck also served as a psychoanalysis specialist.

While practicing psychoanalysis, Aaron Beck took note of the frequency of internal conversation among his clients and noticed how secure the connection was between their feelings and thoughts. Thus, Beck renewed the therapy which he practiced to help his clients to understand, identify, and also deal with the automatic emotion-filled ideas and thoughts which aroused them regularly.

Beck also found that an amalgamation of behavioral techniques and cognitive therapy produced outstanding results. In honing and describing this newly found therapy, Beck was able to lay the foundation for most of the influential and popular treatments.

While this therapy is not made for lifelong participation, it aimed at assisting clients be able to accomplish their objectives within the near future. Many CBT regimens will last for 5 to 10 months, with the clients participating in 50 to 60 minutes sessions.

CBT is a hands-on approach that demands both the client and the therapists to be entirely devoted to the process and also enthusiastic about participating. The client and the therapist must work hand in hand as a group to point out the problems which the client may be facing, come up with efficacious stratagems for solving the challenges and then create positive solutions.

Cognitive Distortions

Majority of the extremely useful and popular CBT techniques are applied to what many scientists and psychologists refer to as cognitive distortions. Cognitive distortions are erroneous thoughts which reinforce negative emotions and thought patterns.

There are 15 central cognitive distortions which can affect the most balanced intellectuals.

1. Filtering

Filtering is a process whereby a person ignores all the great and positive things in life and instead decides to focus on the negative stuff. Filtering is the trap of dwelling on the negative aspects of a given situation, irrespective as to whether a lot of great things surrounds you or not.

2. <u>Polarized Thinking</u>

Polarized thinking is a cognitive distortion where the subject is an all, or nothing thinker will zero room for nuisance or complexity. For these people, everything is either white or black and never gray or shades of grey.

If the person does not perform exceptionally well in certain areas, then they may see themselves as total failures instead of just acknowledging that they might be unskilled in a given area.

3. <u>Overgeneralization</u>

This refers to the taking of a single point in time or incidence and then using the incidence as the main piece of evidence or data for an all-encompassing conclusion. For instance, a person who tends to overgeneralize may forego a critical job interview. This person may brush off the conversation as a bad experience. After trying again, this person will conclude that they are bad at meetings, and thus, they are never going to lead a job.

4. <u>Jumping to Conclusions</u>

Similar overgeneralization, this type of distortion entails defective reasoning on how a person comes up with conclusions. Unlike the overgeneralization distortions, this distortion refers to one's propensity to be sure without any form of evidence. For instance, we may be fully convinced that a person does not like us without any type of real evidence. Alternatively, we may believe that all our dreads may end up coming true before having a chance to really find out.

5. <u>Minimizing or Magnifying/Catastrophizing</u>

This form of distortion entails expecting that the worst has happened or will happen based on an occurrence which is not as cataclysmic as the person made it be. For instance, you might make an insignificant mistake while you are work. Once you make a mistake, you are going to be convinced that this mistake is going to affect the project that you are currently working on. Chances are you also believe that your boss will be furious and thus you might end up losing your role or job.

On the other hand, one may downplay the importance of various essential things, such as accomplishments made at the office or a desired personal quality.

6. <u>Personalization</u>

Personalization is a type of falsification where a person believed that all the things that they do would affect other people or external events, irrespective of how irrational the belief may be. An individual with this type of distortion may feel that they have a role that's exaggerated on all the bad things which tend to transpire around them. For example, a person might believe that coming late for a meeting by a few minutes may lead to the derailment of the meeting and also that everything might have been great if they were able to arrive on time.

7. <u>Control Fallacies</u>

Control fallacy is a type of distortion that entails feeling as if everything which materializes around you is entire because of your actions or some external forces. On certain occasions, some of the things which might happen to use are a result of the effects which we have no control over and on some instances it's because of our actions. Nonetheless, the distortion here is the assumption that it's either one or the other. We may assume that the stubborn co-workers are the one to blame for the imperfect jobs. Alternatively, we could think that the mistake that colleagues make is because of our actions or something that we did.

8. <u>Fallacy of fairness</u>

While we are all anxious about integrity on many occasions, this concern may end up being taken to an extreme. As its widely known, life is not fair at all times. A person who tends to go through life while looking for fairness in every experience is going to end up unhappy and resentful. There are sometimes when things will not go our way, and there are instances when things will go our way.

9. <u>Blaming/Accusations</u>

Applicable when things are not going our ways. We assign the responsibility for the outcomes or try and explain the results. One precise method of transferring the burden is by blaming other people for things that go wrong. There are instances when we are going to blame other people for making us act or feel in a certain way. However, this is a cognitive distortion. Thus, we are entirely responsible for the way we think or act.

10. <u>Should</u>

Should refer to explicit and implicit rules that we have concerning how others or we are supposed to act. When we break the rules that we should live by, we always end up feeling guilty. On the other hand, when other people break the rules that we have set, then we end up being upset. For instance, we might have an unwritten canon those customer representatives are supposed to be accommodating and understanding to the clients. Thus, when we interact with a customer care rep who is discourteous or not accommodating, then we may end up becoming irritated. If we have rules that we are reckless when we spend money on certain things, then we are going always to feel incredibly guilty when we happen to spend some amount of money on these things.

11. Emotional Reasoning

Emotional reasoning is a distortion which entails thinking that if we happened to feel a specific way, then it's true. For instance, we happened to feel uninteresting or unattractive at a given moment, then we will end up thinking that we are uninteresting or unattractive. This cognitive distortion comes down to I sense it, and thus it should be real/authentic. It's clear that our emotions are not on all occasions are suggestive of the truth. However, it can also be difficult to overlook how we genuinely feel.

12 Fallacy of Change

This distortion entails expecting individuals to change to suit us. This distortion ties to the sentiment that our contentment will depend on other folks, their inability or willingness to change. This eventually keeps us from experiencing happiness. This happens to be a detrimental way of thinking since no person is responsible for tour happiness other than you.

13. Mislabeling /Global Labelling

Mislabeling is a cognitive distortion that's an extreme type of generalizing where we generalize a few instances or qualities into a wide range of judgments. For example, if we happen to fail at a specific task, then we may end up coming to the conclusions that we are complete failures in all areas.

On the other hand, when a stranger happens to say something that's somewhat rude, then we may conclude that this individual is a grumpy/unfriendly person. Mislabeling is common to using emotionally loaded and specific language like saying that a mother had abandoned her children when she decided to leave the children under the care of a baby sitter when going to work or attending to specific duties.

14. Always Being Right

This type of distortion tends to make us think and believe that we must always be right, and being wrong cannot be accepted. We may deem that being spot-on is of more importance than other people's feelings, being fair, objective, or admitting that you have made a mistake.

15. Heaven's Reward Fallacy

Is a type of distortion where a person believes that self-denial or sacrifice will eventually pay off. We might consider karma and expect that it will reward us immediately for all the good deeds that we have done. However, many at times, this will result in bitterness when we fail to receive the reward that we were expecting. Majority of the techniques and tools found in CBT are supposed to either reverse or address these cognitive distortions.

9 Elemental CBT Techniques

There are numerous techniques and tools which are used in CBT. Many of the tools can be employed in our day to day lives or a therapy context. The tools and techniques discussed below are some of the most effective and common CBT practices.

Journaling

Journaling is a technique which involves gathering information about a person's thoughts and moods. ACBT journal may include the time of thought and mood, the specific source, the exact reaction, the intensity or extend and a number of other factors. Journaling can assist us in identifying our emotional tendencies and thought patterns, change, describe them cope or adapt.

Unraveling Cognitive Distortion

As a principal objective of CBT, unraveling cognitive distortion can be exercised with the assistance of a therapist or not. To disentangle cognitive distortions, an individual should first ensure that they are aware of the distortions that they suffer from. A part of this will involve identifying and then challenging the harmful and automatic thoughts which fall under any of the categories that we highlighted earlier.

Cognitive Restructuring

Upon the identification of the distortions that is holding you back, then you can always begin to discover how these distortions started and how you began to believe them. Upon finding beliefs which is harmful or destructive then you can always begin the process of challenging the belief.

Does instance, if you tend to believe that you should always have a job that pays well to become somebody respectable and unfortunately you are laid off from a well-paying job, then you are going to start feeling bad and sorry for yourself. However, by accepting the faulty belief which always leads to these types of negative thoughts, then you could be able to take a moment and think about the things which makes you a respectable person, a belief that you might not have thought of unconsidered before.

Response and Exposure Prevention

This type of technique is effective for people who tend to suffer from OCDs. To practice this technique, you will have to expose yourself to the thing that's normally brings about the compulsive behavior. However, to be successful, you will have to be able to refrain from this behavior this time around. You can always decide to combine this technique with journaling, or alternatively employ journaling to fully comprehend how this specific technique tends to make you feel.

Interoceptive Exposure

Interoceptive Exposure is a behavior that's ideal for treating anxiety and panic attacks. This procedure entails the subjection to the feared bodily sensations to as to being out the response. By doing this, we will activate any belief that's unhelpful which is associated with these sensations, maintain the said sensations without any avoidance or distraction and also allow new learning about these sensations to take place. This therapy is intended to assist a person see that the panic symptoms of not pose any threat though they might be uncomfortable.

Rescripting and Nightmare Exposure

Rescripting and nightmare exposure are a form of therapy that's intended specifically for people who tend to suffer from nightmares. Moreover, rescripting treatment therapy is much similar to the interoceptive exposure considering the fact that it elicits the nightmares thereby bring up certain emotions.

Once the emotion is brought to surface, the therapist and the client will work hand in hand and identify the emotion and then come up with a new image that will accompany the emotion that's desired.

Play with the script to the end

This type of technique is very useful for people who suffer from anxiety and fear. Under this technique, the vulnerable person to anxiety and crippling fear is placed under a type of thought experiment where they get to imagine the very worst outcome of a given case scenario.

By allowing the scenario to play out the individuals may be assisted in acknowledging and recognizing that the outcome will always be manageable even if everything that they fear comes

Progressive Muscle Relaxation

Much similar to popular body scan techniques, this technique will instruct the subject on how to relax one of the group of muscles one at time, until the entire body enters into a state of relaxation. Under this approach, you may use a YouTube video, Audio tape or your mind for guidance. This technique can be very helpful when it comes to calming the nerves and soothing a mind that's not only busy but also one that is unfocused.

Relaxed Breathing

Relaxed breathing is also another popular technique which will also resonate well with people who practice mindfulness. There are several ways of relaxing and bringing to regularity to the way that we breath. These can include guided and unguided imagery,

YouTube Videos, audio recordings as well as scripts. Calming our breath and brining regularity to our breathing will allow us to approach a given problem from a balanced place, thereby facilitating more rational and effective decisions.

These techniques may assist individuals who are suffering from a variety of afflictions a d mental illness including OCD depression as well as panic disorders. These techniques may be practiced under the supervision of a psychotherapist or on our own.

To give some of the techniques a try without seeking the assistance of a therapist, you will find handouts and worksheets by the end of the chapter which are going to help you with your practice sessions.

Journaling
Gathering data about your moods, their
source / intensity, and your responses to them.

Unraveling cognitive distortions
Become aware of the distortions you
are likely to be vulnerable of.

Cognitive restructuring
Challenge your harmful or destructive
beliefs and restructure them.

Exposure and response prevention
Expose yourself to whatever it is that
normally provokes a compulsive behavior.

Interoceptive exposure
Exposure yourself to sensations you are
afraid of and recognize they are not dangerous.

Nightmare exposure and rescripting
Identify the emotion caused by a nightmare
and cultivate a new emotion to replace it.

Play the script until the end
Finish a worst case scenario in your head to
see that everything will likely turn out okay.

Progressive muscle relaxation
Relax one muscle group at a time until
your whole body is in a state of relaxation.

Relaxed breathing
Bring regularity and calm to your breath
and create a sense of balance.

Cognitive-behavioral Therapy

If you happen to be a therapist who is looking for several ways that you can use to guide your clients through their treatment or you're just an individual who loves to learn through actions, then there are several CBT worksheets which can always come in very handy.

Coping Styles Worksheet

Coping styles worksheets instruct the instructor and the client to list any of their perceived challenges and difficulty first.

The instructor and the therapist will then work backward while listing the risk factors. You may explain why you are most likely to experience some of these problems other than another person as well as the events or triggers, i.e. the source or stimulus for some of these issues.

Once you have been able to clearly define the problem and then understand why you happen to be struggling with these problems, then the next step would be listing the coping strategies. It's essential to point out that coping stratagems are not solutions to the tribulations that you are facing but rather the ways that we are going to be able to deal with the effects from these problems and the impacts that they are going to have.

The next step would be listing the effectiveness of these surviving strategies, including how they will make you feel in the long-term and short-term as well as the disadvantages and advantages of every approach.

Finally, you will then move to list alternative actions. If the coping strategies are not entirely effective against the exertions, then you are instructed to record different strategies which you believe are going to work much better in comparison to the first.

This type of worksheet is going to get both you a d the client thinking about what you will be currently doing and also what is the best way to take.

ABC Functional Analysis

ABC Functional Analysis is a common technique which helps both you and the client learn more about yourselves, especially what often leads to certain behaviors. ABC also helps us to understand the consequences that are likely to result from these behaviors.

At the middle point of the worksheet, you are going to find a box that's labeled Behaviors. Within this box, you are going to pen down any behavior that you find potentially problematic, and you may want to examine.

On the hand, on the worksheet's left-side, you will find a box which is labeled antecedents, where both you and the client will pen down the factors which ultimately led to the specific conduct under deliberation either indirectly or directly.

On the right side, you will find a table that's labeled Consequences. In this box, you are going to write down what exactly happened after the behavior that's under consideration.

While the term consequences might sound somewhat negative, however, that's not the case. There might be some positive significances which might arise from specific behavior, even if the behavior in question may lead to some negative effects as well.

If you are looking for a great ABC worksheet, then this worksheet will come on handy for you and your client especially when you are trying to establish whether certain behaviors are helpful or adaptive when it comes to striving towards certain goals or self-deafening or destructive.

Case Formulation Worksheet

Under Case Formulation, there are 4 Ps. They include;

- Proposing factors

- Perpetuating factors

- Precipitating factors

- Protective factors

These four factors help us in understanding what might be leading to the arousal of the perceived problem and also what we may be able to do to prevent these problems from being effectively tackled.

In this specific worksheet, the therapist is going to work with the clients through 4 main steps.

First and foremost, the therapist is going to identify the predisposing factors; both the internal or external fact which can contribute to the person developing the perceived issue.

Examples may include life happenings, genetics, or personality. Together, they are going to be combined to help identify the precipitating factors that offer insight into the exact triggers or functions which lead to the emergence of the problem. The next step will be to consider the perpetuating factors to discover the reinforces which might be maintaining the problem.

The final step would be to identify the specific protective factors, to fully understand the strengths of the clients, adaptive behavioral patterns, and social supports.

Extended Case Formulation

This worksheet picks or builds on the previous worksheet. The Extended Case Formulation worksheet will help you and your client to address the 4 P factors which have been described above; protective factors, precipitating, predisposing, and perpetuating. The formulation process will assist you and the client in connecting the dots that are present between our thought patterns, current behavior, and core beliefs.

The Extended Formulation Worksheet will present six boxes which will be found on the page's left side. These boxes should be filled before proceeding to the worksheet's right section.

The first box has been labeled the problem and will correspond with perceived inconveniency that the client might be experiencing. Within the first box, you will be instructed to pen down the stimuli or event which are connected to a specific behavior.

The square that follows is labelled early experiences. It corresponds to the predisposing factors. Under this box, you will be expected to pen down the experiences which you encountered during your childhood that might have contributed to your behavior.

Core beliefs are the third box, which is related to the predisposing factor. In this box, you will be expected to the right some of the most relevant core beliefs that you will have regarding this specific behavior. These refer to the beliefs which might not be explicit but which you might believe deep down within you. They can include notions such as I'm not good enough or I am bad.

Dysfunctional Thought Record

The DTR worksheet is explicitly helpful for individuals who tend to struggle with destructive thoughts and would like to comprehend why and when these thoughts are likely to show up. Getting to know more about what rouses such responses or thoughts makes it much easier to reverse and address them.

This worksheet is apportioned into seven different columns.

Towards the extreme left, you will find a space where you will pen the time and date the dysfunctional thought arose.

In the second column, you will list the situation. You will be asked to describe the specific event which led to the arousal of the dysfunction thought in detail.

On this column, you will be expected to fill in the automatic thought. In this space you will record the dysfunctional thought.

You will also be expected to provide a belief rating on this specific thought on 0 to 100 percent scale.

On the following column, you will list the emotions or emotion that are brought about by this thought. The rating will be filled on an intensity scale that runs from 0 to 100 percent.

You will then use the fifth column to take not of the dysfunctional thought, which is going to be addressed. For instance, maladaptive deliberations will include misrepresentations like overplaying unhelpful events while at the same time dismissing the positives of a given situation or simply overgeneralizing. The Cognitive Distortions Infographics will always come in handy.

In the second last column, you will be expected to pen down alternative thoughts which are more functional and positive to replace the negative thoughts.

Finally, in the last column, the user is expected to pen down the outcomes for the exercise. You will be expected to provide answers for questions such as whether you were able to confront the dysfunctional ideas or thoughts. You will also be expected to pen down an alternative theory that you find quite convincing. You will also be expected to point out whether your belief on the thought or the intensity the emotion decreased.

Fact-Checking

Fact-checking is undeniably one of the most popular CBT tools. This is due to the fact that this tool is helpful when it comes to recognizing the thoughts that are not specifically true. On the top sections of this worksheet, you will find an extremely important lesson: Deliberations are not facts.

At the top of this worksheet is an important lesson: Thoughts are not necessarily facts. While it might be challenging to accept this ideology, especially if we continuously experience intense emotions or dysfunctional thoughts. Taking your time filling this worksheet out will help us realize that ideas are not always facts. This worksheet features 16 statements which the user should ascertain whether they are opinions or facts. The comments may include the following;

- I'm selfish
- I failed the test
- I did not lend my buddy money when they asked for financial assistance.

It's important to point out that this is not in any way a trick. We have the right answers for each of the 17 statements. If you are wondering, then the right answers for the statements mentioned above are as follows (belief, truth, truth).

This straightforward exercise is going to assist the user in being able to realize that while we might have several psychologically charged deliberations, not all of these thoughts are objective truths. Acknowledging the difference between opinions and facts will help us in fighting the harmful and dysfunctional notions which we might have about ourselves or other people.

Cognitive Restructuring

The cognitive restructuring worksheet employs the Socratic questioning. The Socratic Questioning is a technique that can assist the user in challenging a variety if illogical and irrational thoughts.

On the first page of this worksheet, you will find a suggestion for What are you thinking. The client or the psychologists might make use of his space to pen down a particular thought which you suspect is irrational or destructive.

Next, you will then pen down the specifics which contradict or support this specific thought making thereby making it a reality. What are some of the facts about this thought that are accurate? What facts call this thought into action? Once you have been able to identify the evidence, you can now make use of the last box on this specific thought to come up with a judgment for this particular thought, primarily whether the idea is based on specific evidence or it's just merely your opinion.

On the page that follows, you are going to find a Socratis Questions mind map that you can use to challenge your thoughts or train of thoughts much further. You might opt to rewrite, what are you thinking at the center so that it will be much easier to challenge the specific ideas with the questions.

One of the questions inquires whether the questions are purely a black or white situation which has no grey areas. This is where you are going to think about and then write down whether you will be making use of the all-or-nothing thinking, for instance. Moreover, this question will also allow you to assess whether you are making things comprehensible when they are amazingly complex.

Another question will inquire whether you might be misapprehending the evidence presented or making unverified assumptions. As it is the case with all, the bubbles, penning it down is going to make the exercise much more effectual.

A third bubble will instruct you to contemplate on whether other folks might have different interpretations of similar situations. Also, you will be asked to think whether you have an idea what those interpretations may be.

You are then going inquire whether you are examining at all the proof or you are just looking at the evidence which supports the belief that you already have. Try and be as unbiased as you can.

Moreover, it helps to inquire whether your specific thoughts are inflation of the truth. On many occasions, we tend to experience some destructive thoughts which apparently are not based on any facts.

You will also be instructed to examine whether you are entertaining negative thoughts because of a habit you developed or whether there are realistic evidences which support these thoughts.

You will then have to think about the origin of this specific thought. Was the idea passed over by someone else? If the thought or idea was passed over by another person, was the individual a reliable person or a person who is not to be trusted?

Finally, you will have to complete the worksheet by identifying the scene that your thoughts/assumptions are likely to bring up and what would the worst-case scenario look like.

The Socratic questions will encourage the participant to take a deep dive into their thoughts a d thought processes which plague them and then offer opportunities to evaluate and analyze these thoughts. If your thoughts do not come from a place of actuality, then a Cognitive-Restructuring Worksheet will be a great tool of recognizing and eliminating these thoughts.

More CBT Exercises and Interventions.

If you are yet to use any CBT Tools or techniques, then you should definitely read on as we provide extremely effective exercises that will be useful when brain training.

Behavioral Experiments

Behavioral experiments relate to thought experiments. These types of analyses tend to differ entirely from thought experimentations because they test out the 'What Ifs' out of your thoughts.

To test a specific thought, you can decide to experiment with the outcomes from several thoughts. For instance, you can choose to test out the following ideas, 'If I happen to criticize myself, then I am going to work extremely hard on myself vs. If I happen to be kind to myself, then I am going to work much harder'.

First, you are going to try and criticize yourself when you required motivation to work much harder and take note of the results. After that, you are then going to try and be kind to yourself and then take note of the results.

The next would now be comparing the results to establish which thought was much closer to the truth. The behavioral experiments to test our beliefs will assist us in learning how to attain our therapeutic goals and also how we can be able to be the best versions of ourselves.

Thought Records

These are beneficial methods of testing the validity of our thoughts. Thought Records involve the collection and evaluation of evidence for and also against a specific theory, thereby allowing a conclusion that's evidence-based. The conclusion will help us determine whether our thoughts are valid or not.

For instance, you might be having the belief that "My buddy thinks that I am not a great friend. For this case, you may want to think about the substantiation for this specific belief like my friend did not pick up the phone the last time I called her or the friend decided to cancel your weekend plan on the last minute.

You might also want to look at the evidence that's against this belief such as, the friend calls you back after failing to answer your call or she decided to invite you to a barbeque the following weekend. If the friend thought that you were a bad friend, then she would not have invited you over.

Upon collecting the evidence against and for, the goal would now to come up with thoughts that are more stable like, "My associate is a busy person, and therefore she is not always going to answer my call every time. If I understand this, then I am going to be a truly great friend.

The thought records apply to the use of logic to fight off much harmful and unreasonable thoughts and then replace these thoughts with the ones that are more rational and balanced.

Pleasant Activity Scheduling

Pleasant Activity Scheduling is a technique which can be extremely helpful when addressing depression. It entails the scheduling of activities within the near future that you can always look forward to.

Essentially, you might want to pen down at least one activity each day so that you will be able to engage in this activity in the week. The event can include watching a film or series that you excited about or calling a friend so that you can catch up with them. It could be anything which you find pleasant, providing it's not unhealthy i.e. smoking or consuming an entire cake.

You might also try coming with a schedule for a particular activity for every day, which provides a sense of great accomplishment. It is a fantastic way of doing something pleasant, however doing something small which may make us feel more accomplish might have far-reaching and long-lasting effects.

This straightforward procedure may present more positivity into our lives, and the Pleasant Activity Worksheet will help you do that.

Imagery -Based Exposure

This type of exercise entails thinking about one of your most recent memories which created powerful and negative emotions and then carefully analyze the situation.

For instance, you had a fight recently with your spouse, and they happened to say something that you found quite harmful, you can always bring the situation to your mind and then try and recall it in exact details. After that, you will then have to try and label the thoughts and emotions that you experienced during the occasion. You will also have to identify the urges that you felt i.e., tell your partner or run away or cry.

By envisaging this bad situation or experience, especially for a prolonged period, it will help you get rid of the trigger's ability and then reduce it through coping. When you decide to expose yourself to all of the urges and feelings that you experienced and survive through them, then you are going to take away some of its powers. A worksheet will prove to be quite useful for this activity.

Graded-Exposure Worksheet

While this method may sound somewhat complicated, it is not. Creating a situation exposure entails listing the situations that you believe might be avoided. For instance, a person who suffers from severe public/social anxiety might avoid asking a person out on a date or making a phone call.

The next step would be to rate each of the items on the level of distress that you would experience from 0 to 10 if you decided to engage in the activity. For a person who is suffering from extreme social/public anxiety asking a person out on a date might receive a rating of 10 on this scale. On the other hand, making a phone call may receive a rating of 3 or 4.

Upon rating the situations, you are now going to rank these situations by This will assist you in recognizing what are some of the most significant difficulties that you might be facing and also will assist you in deciding what items you are going to solve first and the order that you should solve. It's highly advisable to always begin with the things that are least stressing and then work up to the most distressing items.

CBT Workbook and Manual for Practice

If you are more than interested in trying out CBT with your clients, then there are several manuals and books which will contain useful information that will help you get started.

A percentage of these books are supposed to be used by therapists alone, while others are to be explored with a team or with the supervision or guidance of a psychoanalyst.

There are hundreds of manuals on the market that will assist therapists in applying CBT in their line of work. You can Google the works of Jeffrey A. Cully, Ricardo F. Munoz, and Guillermo Bernal.

Several other workbooks and manuals are available on the market and will assist us in starting out with CBT. However, the tools listed above are a fantastic place to start.

Cognitive Behavioral Activities

There are several CBT exercises and activities which might prove helpful to you and your clients, and thus we would like to look at them.

Mindfulness Meditation

Meditation/mindfulness has many positive effects, including fighting addiction problems, anxiety, depression, anxiety, and other types of mental illness. This approach can also assist those people who are suffering from extremely serious deliberations to separate from obsession and rumination by helping them to stay firmly ground in the current.

Successive Approximation

While it has a fancy name, Successive Approximation is a simple idea which you might have already encountered before. It entails the breaking down of huge tasks into small manageable tasks or steps.

It might be quite overwhelming to address a huge goal, such as remodeling a house or opening a business. This can also be the case when it comes to mental health treatment since the main aim is to overcome anxiety, depression, and even attain mental wellness which might appear to be a monumental mission.

By breaking down the vast goals into small and easy to realize steps, we will be a le to come up with a success path and in turn, make our journey to be less overwhelming.

Penning Down Statements to Counter Negative Thoughts

Unlike the other three techniques, this one can prove to be somewhat problematic for someone who is still fresh to CBT therapy or a person who might be suffering from extreme symptoms. While it might be difficult, this technique, when appropriately employed, can be beneficial.

On occasions when negative thoughts plague you, then it might prove to be quite tricky overcoming these thoughts, especially if you strongly believe in these contemplations.

To fight these negative deliberations, it might be beneficial to list down a thought that's not only opposite but also positive.

For instance, if a negative thought such as I am worthless keeps on appearing on your brain, then you can try to pen down a statement such as I am an essential person or I am somebody with potential.

At first, it might be somewhat difficult to accept the replacement thoughts that you would have created fully. However, the more you end up bringing up the new and positive deliberations to offset the negative thoughts, then the higher the association will end up being.

Visualize the beautiful parts of the day

Once you begin feeling either negatively or become depressed, it can be quite difficult to acknowledge or remember that there are various aspects of our lives which are positive.

This straightforward procedure of bringing the significant parts of our lives or day to the surface might be taking a lesser step in the correct direction, which entails acknowledging the positive.

All you will have to do is to pen down some of the things in your life that you are grateful for. Alternatively, you could also pen down some of the positive events which happened at any given day. A simple act of penning down these great things will help you forge new wirings in your brain which will in turn make it much easier for the brain to see positives even if you happen to be experiencing negative thoughts.

Reframe all negative deliberations

It can be straightforward to give in to all the negative thoughts. If you happen to find your brain generating negative thoughts when you come across something new, then you should try and reframe your mind. For instance, you might enter a new room and then say to your inner self that I hate the color that had been used on the wall.

Reframing your mind will involve countering all the negative thoughts by taking note of things which tend to make you feel positive as quickly as possible. For example, in the case that we gave earlier, where you find yourself hating the color of the room, you might push your brain to take note of at least five things in the place which you feel are attractive or positive about. For example, you could take note of the carpet or open the windows and enjoy the sunshine that they bring into the room.

You can also decide to set your phone in such a manner that it will remind you throughout the day to take a break and stop whatever you are doing and then begin to take note of all the positive things that are around you.

Doing this will assist you in pushing all the negative thoughts deep down and then instead focus on the positive.

Chapter 6

Mindfulness and the Brain

Have you at any given point in time felt overwhelmed, stressed, or anxious?

We all live in a hectic world. With texts and email notifications constantly buzzing our phones, deadlines approaching fist, running errands at home while stepping over toys, trying to feed the pets as our food is getting cold, chances are we will all end feeling quite stressed out each day.

As luck would have it, there is a straightforward exercise that you can always employ to calm yourself down naturally and be able to appreciate life more.

It's known as mindfulness.

We all have heard of the term mindfulness; however, what exactly does this term mean when relating to the brain and in the field of neuroscience?

Existing in the present moment is hugely encouraging. It means focusing all your awareness on now and here. It's all about embracing every moment of our days and now having to worry about what tomorrow might bring.

Living in the current and present moment may prove to a transformative experience. However, what exactly does live in the present have to do with our brains?

The human brain contains trillions of synapses which assist the cells found in our minds to correspond with each other. The human brain contains around 80-100 billion neurons, all of which are a more significant part of these connections.

Despite everything, scientists and researchers still do not have a clear understanding of what exactly happens within the human brain when practicing meditation or mindfulness.

The knowledge that currently exists about the human brain is so limited because from the look of things is that there is so much to learn.

In this chapter, we are going to look at mindfulness, the research in this field, and the studies. Moreover, we are also going to look at how mindfulness changes and affects the human brain.

In recent years, researchers began looking at how mindfulness may help with conditions such as autism and ADHD, which is extremely exciting.

Therefore, what exactly is mindfulness?

Mindfulness refers to the practice of explicitly fixing all our focus on the present moment and then accepting the moment without any judgment. This is a fantastic place to begin, especially if you are keen on finding the key to happiness.

When executed correctly, mindfulness is going to allow us to lessen our anxiety and stress levels, reduce the time that we spend feeling quite overwhelmed and also assist you in appreciating every special moment as it takes place. In a universe that's filled with bedlam, mindfulness may be a trick that we need to study to be able to put up with the insanity that's always around us.

If you would love to experience these outcomes, then we highly recommend that you continue reading through this guide to becoming mindful throughout your day.

Research on Mindfulness

There are a variety of studies that have been conducted on mindfulness. A few widely acknowledged examinations include Mindfulness-Based brain Therapy (MBCT) and Mindfulness-Based Stress Reduction.

· The MBSR was fashioned by Jon Kabat-Zin and his team at the world-renowned medical center of the University of Massachusetts.

· The MBCT was created by Teasdale, Segal, and Williams.

MBSR is a program that was created to help people with pain, several life issues, and a wide range of conditions. Many of these issues might be challenging to deal primarily within the hospital setting. It has also been established that the MBSR course also plays a crucial role in alleviating stress, depression, chronic pain, and anxiety. The course combines mindful movement and cognitive behaviors with meditation techniques. This course is taught in a manner that's not only practical but also relevant to the everyday setting.

The course is an excellent example of how becoming mindful can assist us with several things going beyond just relaxing the body and mind and also being present. The main goal of MBCT is to help people to change unproductive thoughts. This may include tough patterns which are not serving us well or different types of emotional responses and behaviors.

Moreover, MBCT also uses several psychological techniques which can assist patients to understand better the correlation that's present between mood disorders and the mind. When you acknowledge the connection, you will be able to work towards an appropriate answer. You can be able to make use of the secure connection that's present between pain and mind to alter the way that we think.

This type of therapy is believed to be helpful, especially when recovering from depression and anxiety that's related to pain. MBCT borrows significantly from MBSR structure. It also integrates some approaches from CBT. It's taught in a format that takes an eight-week form that will include up to 12 participants.

MCBT program is going to include;

Cultivation of consciousness through a mindfulness exercise.

A framework consisting of acceptance, non-striving, and an authentic interest in know-how that's assimilated into the teaching process.

A process that links learning methods with the understanding of how to work with the concept or idea of vulnerability.

Personal experimental learning is incorporated into a broader outline of understanding. The understanding relates to the general human vulnerability nature and suffering to the specific kind of the vulnerability and depressive lapses.

The sessions are accelerated through reflection, dialogue, teaching, and group exercises. While mindfulness-based brain therapy might be somewhat imposing, the meaning is quite straightforward.

M-Refers to r bringing your consciousness to the existing and present without any expectations of judgments. (mindfulness).

B- Based or connected to or derived from

C- Cognitive-refers to the planning, thinking, and measuring different parts of our brains.

T- Therapy/Treatment of diseases and ailments.

CBT happens to be one of the well respected and highly recommended talk therapies of the century. Scientists define CBT as a directive, time-limited, active and structure approach which is used in the treatment of several mental problems such as phobias, depressions, pain and stress. CBT is a treatment whether the client gets to choose their own goals.

Moreover, CBT focuses on the now and here just like MBCT. Within the Academic community, there are several mindfulness researchers that you should be aware of including David Creswell, Larissa DUNCAN, Elissa Epel, and Judson Brewer.

Studies that you should know about

According to researchers and scientists, mindfulness changes the human brain. Dunne, Davidson, and Lutz looked at how mindfulness affects the amygdala, which happens to be the region of the brain, which is related to emotional processes.

Within this study, it was established that this region of the brain appeared to have less activity as well as less gray matter density right after mindfulness sessions. Another part of the brain that plays a crucial role in mindfulness is hippocampus. The hippocampus is a section of the human brain that's linked to memory. It also helps normalize the amygdala. Right after mindfulness training, it was established that this section of the brain was even more active.

According to another study which was conducted at the University of North Carolina, mindfulness can assist us in nurturing healthier relationships. This study demonstrated that there was a correlation between improved relationship and the mindfulness practice. In the study, couples reported that they not only experienced more closeness, but they also experienced more satisfaction, to name but a few

There are other studies which examined the brain's prefrontal cortex, which is p[art of the human brains that's associated with maturity and impulse control. This section of the brain became more active right after mindfulness training.

In a different study which was published by NeuroReport in the year 2005, the results showed that the thicker cortical sections which related to sensory and attention procession in long-standing meditation in comparison with those of people who did not meditate.

The findings also suggested that simple practices of meditation might offset the thinning of the cortex that's brought about due to aging.

Another `analysis of the MBSR study for medical practitioners indicated that the mindfulness practice of the nurses enabled empathetic attitudes while at the same time decreasing the tendency of the nurses to pick up the negative emotions of other people.

Proven Benefits

According to the research, mindfulness can assist us in improving in many ways especially within the workplace environment. Christopher Liddy, a doctoral candidate at the Case Western School, undertook research alongside an assistant professor at the Pepperdine University, one Darren Good.

Their research looked at more than 4, 000 scientific papers on various degrees of mindfulness. Moreover, the researchers also examined the influence of mindfulness when it comes to how people feel, think, and perform while at work.

The result of this study was then published in the Management Journal. It was titled, Contemplating Mindfulness at Work.

This study suggests the following;

1. Mindfulness has a positive impact on human functioning.

2. Mindfulness will assist you in improving the quality of your attention

3. Even though it happens to be an internal quality, mindfulness can aid in interpersonal behavior.

4. Mindfulness helps provide better compassion and empathy.

In this research, it was established that mindfulness not only has a positive impact on our attention, it also helps to improve our emotions, cognition, behavior, and physiology. The two researchers also discovered that mindfulness would help in keeping our attention stable, thereby allowing us to remain focused on the present. Individuals who were able to successfully complete mindfulness training could stay focused and vigilant, especially while undertaking listening and visual tasks.

It has also been established that mindfulness can help improve the three unique attention qualities, including efficacy, control, and stability. On the other hand, when it comes to relationships, mindfulness may encourage us, thereby helping us to provide compassion and empathy.

According to Davin, apart from being a formidable tool for patients, mindfulness is a tremendous tool for medical care practitioners and doctors. There are several benefits associated with mindfulness including;

1. Optimization of a person's mental health

2. Treatment of chronic pain

3. Treatment of insomnia

4. Positive impact on our immune system and the brain

5. Aid with caregiver burnout that many health caregivers might face.

In a review which included more than 20 randomized control trials, it was established that mindfulness could assist in the improvement of our overall mental health. The study also revealed that mindfulness could aid in the mitigation of relapse risks resulting from depression. It also helps in the treatment of disorders such as PTSD. On top of that, it was established that mindfulness also helps to boost our immune system and also improve neural processing in sessions that last between 10 to 15 minutes.

The research also revealed that mindfulness played a significant role when it came to depression. Since chronic pain is an epidemic, it's essential to come up with other tools that which are drug-free and mindfulness happens to be one of those tools. In this study, it was established that the people who mediated displayed a decrease in pain-related confines. The benefits of the study were similar to those of cognitive-behavioral therapy.

Poor sleeping pattern and insomnia may also lead to several health problems. In several randomized controlled tests, it was discovered that mindfulness could help lessen insomnia.

This meant that mindfulness could be of great benefit to healthcare workers. Burnout is a significant problem among healthcare industry, and thus the studies indicated that mindfulness could help create favorable chances and boost resilience while at the same time reducing anxiety, burnout, and stress among employees especially those working with the healthcare industry.

Neuroscience of Mindfulness

From the discussion above, we have seen the benefits that mindfulness brings. Apart from helping us to cope better, mindfulness also helps our brains to perform and function much better. Neuroplasticity allows our brains to restructure themselves. Neuroplasticity achieves this by creating new neural connections throughout our life. Numerous research and studies show that mindfulness will help us improve our resilience, thereby allowing us to cope much better.

Through the application of neuroplasticity, we can rewire and hardwire our brains, which will help us attain higher levels of happiness, joy, peace, and health. A Harvard Medical School, neuroscientist, Sara Lazar uses MRI equipment to study the brain. In her study, Lazar looks at the comprehensive brain structures to establish what is happening when performing specific tasks such as yoga or meditation.

At first, Lazar was a skeptic. However, everything changed when she decided to attend yoga sessions. After a few classes, Lazar began to feel the difference. Apart from feeling happier, Lazar also felt calmer and more compassionate. Because of this experience, Lazar decided to redeploy her research/study on the specific changes which occur within the brain's physical structure because of meditation practice.

In her first study, Lazar looked at people who had far-reaching meditation experience. This study involved focusing on inner experiences. The data collected showed that extensive mediation prevented or slowed down the thinning of the frontal cortex due to aging. This is the area of the brain which contributes to memory formation,

Many people assume that humans become oblivious as they age. However, Lazar established that individuals who meditated in their 50's or 40's had similar amounts of the brain's grey matter as individuals who are in their 30's and 20's. in her second study, Lazar used individuals who had never meditated. This group of people was asked to attend a mindfulness-based stress-reduction program. The participants took a one-week class. This group of people was also invited to participate in several mindfulness exercises, including body scan exercises, mindful yoga, and sitting meditation.

The sessions/exercises lasted for about 30 to 40 minutes each day. In this specific study, Lazar tested the participants for the positive outcomes that the mindful meditation was going to have on their psychological well-being. Sara Lazar also had interest in helping relieve symptoms of insomnia, depression, nervousness and chronic pain.

Eight weeks later, the volume of their brain had increased in four different regions. Of these regions, the most relevant include;

- Temporoparietal junction
- Hippocampus

The areas of the brain which decreased included the amygdala structure.

The hippocampus is a brain structure which is fashioned like a seahorse. This region is accountable for, learning, regulation of emotions, storage of memories, and spatial orientation. On the other hand, the temporoparietal junction is the region where parietal lobes convene with the temporal area. This is the area of the brain which is responsible for compassion and empathy.

This study also showed that there was a reduction in the size of the amygdala, which in turn meant that fight/flight response and reaction to threats reduces significantly.

The lesser the size of the amygdala, the better the person can cope or react to stress. According to another study, the decrease brain's grey matter correlates with changes on stress levels.

From these studies, we can deduce that a change in a change in people's responses occurs within their inner selves and not within the surrounding environment. In the long, mindfulness can assist us in changing how we react to stressful situations, thereby helping us to feel calmer and take control.

How mindfulness Changes and Affects the Brain

In the last ten years, studies and research in the field of neuroimaging looked at specific changes in the human brain about mindfulness meditation.

One analysis that was taken from more than 21 neuroimaging studies looked at the brains of more than 300 experienced meditation practitioners. The research revealed that eight different regions of the human brain in people who experience meditation were changed consistently changed.

The eight regions of the brain entailed

- Corpus callosum
- Mid-cingulate cortex
- Insular cortex
- Rostro lateral prefrontal cortex
- Sensory cortices
- Hippocampus
- Anterior cingulate cortex
- Superior longitudinal fasciculus

It's important to point out that the exact manner in which these regions of the brain changed, varied from one study to the other since each study used differed neuroimaging measurements. Nonetheless, consistent fluctuations were noted including;

- Changes in the thickness of the brain tissue

- Changes in the density of the brain
- Changes in the surface area of the cortical.
- Changes in the density of the white matter fiber

When reviewing this exploration, we can note a positive trend, especially with those who practice mindfulness and practice meditation.

The Role of Each Unique Region of the Brain

The first region of the brain that we are going to look at is the rostro lateral prefrontal cortex, which is a region of the human brain that's linked with the processing of complex and abstract information, introspection and greater awareness of the thinking process.

The insular cortex and sensory cortex are regions of the brain which happen to be the central cortical hub, especially dealing with tactile information such as body awareness, pain, conscious perception, and touch. The hippocampus, on the other hand, is a set of subcortical structures which are involved with the creation of memories and the facilitation of emotional responses.

The mid-cingulate cortex and the anterior cingulate cortex are the regions of the brain which are connected with the regulation of emotions, attention, and self-control.

Corpus callosum and superior longitudinal fasciculus are what is known as the white matter expanses. These regions communicate within between the brain's hemispheres. Researchers and scientists suggest that the impact of meditation on the brain structures is of medium magnitude. The outcome can be compared to the effect of other intervention like education, behavioral intervention, and psychological interventions.

Because this specific study involved several regions of the human brain, researchers, and scientists that the impact of meditation on the human brain may include a variety of aspects of the human brain function on a bigger scale, which is extremely promising.

Because of this research, Holzel, Posner, and Tang suggest that partaking in mindfulness activities and practice is very promising especially when it comes to the treatment of medical disorders, enhanced we-being and creating of a healthy mind.

Research with meditation and mindfulness is still in its early stages. However, even with this being the case, several studies looked at changes in the activation of the human brain while handling specific tasks and while at rest. To better understand the processes, the studies were conducted on people who practiced mindfulness meditation.

Mindfulness vs. Medication

There are several promising kinds of research and studies when it comes to equating medication to mindfulness therapies. In a recent trial, the researchers compared MBCT with antidepressant medication. After the survey was completed, the result showed that among the participants who had an unpredictable remission, 73 percent of these group had a significant reduction in the risk of experiencing relapse on both the antidepressant and MBCT in comparison to the placebo.

On the other hand, there was no notable difference between the depressant and the MBCT groups. The results from this group are incredibly encouraging because they suggest that MBCT is an excellent alternate treatment to medication.

The people who used MBCT were able to work on developing their capacities and even on their coping strategies so that they would be able to view their deliberations and thoughts differently, in a bigger and broader way. Thus, as a result, these people were able to develop more self-compassion, which in turn assisted them in meditating MBCT's efficacy.

According to research conducted by Brensilver, the use of antidepressants has grown tremendously throughout the years.

In the year 2000, only 6 percent of the entire world population used antidepressants. However, in the year 200, the number rose to 10.4 percent. Both mindfulness and meditation have a similar goal. Reduce the quantity of distress that a person experience.

We have different ideologies when these interventions. For some individuals settling for antidepressants allows them to feel much more stabilized, which then allows them to focus better on a practice like mindfulness. It has been proved that combining psychotherapy and medication often results in better outcomes, unlike using any of these alone.

The same may be said for combining meditation and mindfulness with antidepressants. This will always result in a much better outcome. According to the researcher, psychiatric medication is not usually designed to assist a person to flourish or thrive. The researcher suggests that mindfulness offers something precious and distinctive.

In his opinion, Brensilver suggests that mindfulness not only helps to lessen distress, but it also leads the person to a state of mind where they will be able to flourish. With this state of mind, the person will be able to develop a profound completeness of the present moment.

Benefits of mindfulness

Mindfulness reduces overthinking and rumination

Also known as rumination, overthinking is undeniably one of the most common symptoms which come with anxiety. Once a person begins to worry about something, then their brain is going to hold on tightly into the thought and then make it extremely difficult to dismiss this thought.

Thus, it's quite easy to fall into a loop, where you constantly replay all the bad outcomes that outcome that you could imagine. We all understand deep down that this cannot be useful in any way because continually worrying about something is not going to prevent that thing from occurring.

One study on mindfulness showered that individuals who were yet to engage in mindfulness, began to display less signs of anxiety and rumination in comparison to the control groups upon their introduction to mindfulness.

Mindfulness alleviates stress

Because people are generally confronted with an ever-increasing level of pressure due to society's multifaceted nature, people are often overwhelmed with high levels of stress. This will eventually contribute to several other health problems. Mindfulness tends to help the reduction of importance since it acts as a preventive measure. It also helps people manage to get swiftly through the most challenging times.

Mindfulness improves concentration, performance, and memory concentrating on the task that you are currently working on and paying attention might be one the most noteworthy cognitive abilities that individuals have. Mindfulness is among the few approaches which tend to work as an antidote for the adverse effects and mind-wandering, which may result from the loss of concentration.

As a matter of fact, research which was conducted on students showed that there is a strong association between paying attention in the classroom and mindfulness.

More studies have also shown that by meditating regularly will cause the cerebral cortex of the brain, the part that's accountable for concentration, learning, and memory to thicken.

Mindfulness aids with emotive reactivity
Of the reasons which people tend to have for getting to know more about meditation, being less reactive emotional will be high on their list. Zen or being mindful will always equate to move away from the punches that life throws at you and in the process becoming non-reactive to some of the things which might come

along your way. The study of mindfulness has allowed the participants of various studies to distance their emotional response from various upsetting features and instead focus more on cognitive tasks in comparison to control groups.

Mindfulness encourages cognitive flexibility

There is a study which suggests that mindfulness will not only help people to become less volatile but will also give individuals more intellectual flexibility. Individuals who practice mindfulness tend to have the ability to practice self-observation that instinctively disjoin the paths formed in the brain before learning. It also allows info which is happening at present to be clearly understood in an exciting and novel way.

Meditation stimulates the section of the human brain, which is commonly linked with an adaptive reaction to stress. After being negatively reacted, this region corresponds to a fast recovery.

Mindfulness leads to better-off relationships

Researchers and scientists are still not sure whether this truly works. However, budding brain studies/researches have revealed that individuals who engage in the activity of mindfulness regularly display functional and structural changes within the brain regions which are interrelated to heightened compassion, kindness, and compassion?

Another significant benefit of mindfulness is the effect which it has on the amygdala, the section of the brain that's known as the emotional processing heart. Mindfulness tends to results in the reductions of amygdala's volume and also the connection that it has with the prefrontal cortex. This, in turn, suggests that mindfulness as a process may support decreased reactivity and emotion regulation, which happen to be the two most important instruments for maintaining and creating relationships.

Mindfulness reduces apprehension/anxiety

Science and study have shown that mindfulness is especially helpful when it comes to reducing stress. By practicing mindfulness regularly, the process will help revamp your brain so that you can be able to redeploy your attention. Instead of following a thought that's not only negative but also worrying down a path which has lots of possible outcomes, you can be able to learn how to acknowledge our feelings for what they are genuinely are or let these thoughts go.

Mindfulness improves sleep quality

Relaxation response which your body receives after mindful mediation tends to be quite the opposite of what the body experiences after responding to stress. This type of relaxation response tends to work to ease several health issues that are related to stress such as high blood pressure, depression, and pain. Many sleep disorders are related to these types of ailments,

A study which was conducted on various aging adults confirms that this meditation can assist us in getting quality sleep. Another study reveals that mindfulness meditation has the ability to increase meditation response through mindfulness function of increasing a person's attentional factors which have an impact over the automatic nervous system.

Mindfulness improves mental health

Scientists and researchers have been able to establish that IBMT tends to begin positive structural changes within the human brain which can help in the protection of mental diseases. Practicing mindfulness will help to boost the efficiency in sections of the brain, which help people in regulating their behaviors.

Mindfulness offers pain relief

More than 100 million Americans tend to suffer from long-lasting pain. However, 40-70 percent of these individuals are not getting appropriate medical care. Several studies and research have shown that mindfulness could aid in the reduction of pain without necessarily having to use any types of endogenous-opioid structures which are considered to have the ability to reduce pain during techniques such as mindfulness.

The self-generated opioid systems have always been believed to be the significant part of the human brain for mitigating pain without using drugs. The system produces three types of opioids entailing leuenkephalin's met, dynorphins and beta-endorphin.

Enhances sex life

Studies show that mindfulness has the ability of improving the sex life of a woman by silencing any mental conversation that may be crisscrossing their minds and prevent them from experiencing or enjoying the present sexual impetuses. This can also come on handy in the sex life of a man as well.

Mindfulness increases patience and resilience.

According to one study, Lama Oser's (the man who worked as Dalai Lama's assitant) prefrontal action ratio was extremely high in comparison to a sample that was collected from 175 people. This piece of information indicated that Lama had high levels of well-being, equanimity as well as the resilience to any form of negativity that could be traced back to his adherence of mindfulness.

Decelerates the progression of neurodegenerative disorders

Studies have established that the positive changes within the brain are linked with mindfulness meditation which has been known to reduce anxiety and stress levels in our bodies. Mindful meditation might work to slow down the advancement of several cognitive disorders that are age-related like Dementia and Alzheimer's.

Patients who were suffering from the Alzheimer's disease partook in a study showed some levels of decline in cognitive functions after participating in a two-month mindfulness-based program in comparison to a group which did not partake in this study.

Mindfulness increases creativity

Inventiveness will require an individual to have a balance between the brain's control network and its freestyle network. By balancing control and freestyle with self-expression you will always produce innovative results. The regular practice of mindfulness is an integral part of coming up with this balance.

Different researchers have also deliberated on the effects of two meditation exercises on the convergent and divergent way of thinking. They were able to establish that mindful meditation tends to improve these ways of thinking significantly.

Mindfulness reduces loneliness

There is more to isolation other than having a lack of companionship of living in a silent house. As time goes by, isolation will have a significant impact on our overall psyche as well as our physical wellbeing.

These feelings of loneliness have all been linked with an increase in anxiety, depression, Alzheimer's disease, and a short lifespan. This, in turn, implies that it's incredibly imperative to come up with effective treatment alternatives for people living in isolation.

There is a study which looked at a group of 40 grown-ups and found out that reflecting for at least ½ an hour every day for a total of 8 weeks reduced the participant's feeling of loneliness.

Mindfulness meditation diminishes race bias and implicit age. Research has shown that mindfulness has the ability to positively changing any negative associations and thoughts that we might have. The effect of mindfulness was looked at in favor to numerous biases through the measurements of subjective association tests. In these tests, it was found that individuals who took their time to listen to mindfulness mediation experienced an increase in their mindfulness state and a decline in their potential prejudices.

Mindfulness boosts body satisfaction

Mindful meditation entails self-compassion minus any form of judgment and full acceptance. Mindfulness encourages a non-judgmental and non-striving view of the universe. When individuals are not satisfied with their physiques, they fail to experience any form of satisfaction, mainly because of their obsession with their bodies or appearance.

A study undertaken in the year 2014, distributed the participants who were all women to a control group or medical intervention. The women who were in the intervention-group got to experience three self-compassion training weeks, mainly through meditation. The group of women got to experience a significant reduction in body shame, body dissatisfaction as well as contingent self-worth based on their overall appearance. They also got to experience more significant gains in body appreciation and self-compassion in comparison to the women who were in the control groups. Astonishingly, the women were still able to feel these outstanding positive effects three months down the line.

Mindfulness augments the ability to recover and deal with illness When people think of meditation or mindfulness, they usually think of private peacetime. Conversely, when people think of either the doctor's office or hospital, they tend to think about pain, anxiety, and chaos all around them. Therefore, how exactly can mindfulness be introduced into health care?

eCALM is a therapy program that's designed specifically for people who have cancer. The trial found that mindfulness had the ability to reduce physical indications of stress, reduce a person's emotional reactivity to undesirable experiences as well as enable post-traumatic growth while at the same time relieving fatigue and enhancing energy.

Moreover, another study discovered that mindfulness meditation also had the ability to foster traumatic emotional and mental growth in survivors of breast cancer and also increase spirituality and energy as well.

Mindfulness assists students to attain academic success
Every person knows that apart from prospering academically, people also want young people to physically well and be happy. All these objectives are well connected. We have now realized that emotional and social well-being has a critical role in attaining academic success. Teaching ourselves how to focus on a person's attention on productive tasks, stay inspired and even become more self-aware, be able to deal with frustration and communicate with our peers are all vital skills which depend on the student's ability to understand and even manage their feelings/emotions.

Scientists and researchers found out that scholars who were able to learn the art of mindfulness had the ability to perform much better in their respective verbal reasoning section of GRE. Moreover, these students also got to experience improvements within their working memories. While most debates on school reforms highlight the importance of academic achievement, important movements are created each day by the people who manage to take holistic and complete approaches to education.

Mindfulness assist in the lowering of turnover or burnout at work The earliest reports of job burnout first came out during the 1970s. These reports mostly came from people who were working on human services and the health care sectors. While the research on job burnout is continuously growing, there is not agreed-upon definition that has been agreed upon. While this is the case, job burnout refers to a person's inability to respond to chronic occupation stress, because they are experiencing depersonalization, emotional exhaustion, and low personal achievement rates.

Work exhaustion can manifest as aggression, depression, diminished cognitive performance, lessened motivation, and decreased commitment. This ideology has been widely linked with an amplified risk of mental and physical problems like heart diseases, depression, anxiety, and increased blood pressure. There is a study which found out that there exists an inverted relationship between the job turnover intention and mindfulness, suggesting that their employees who have been trained in mindfulness have fewer chances of quitting their jobs due to any reason.

With that said, this is the main benefits of mindfulness. Out of all the benefits discussed below, which one would you like to experience? After looking at the key benefits of mindfulness, let us now dive into the practice of mindfulness during the day.

Mindfulness 101: Practicing Mindfulness

There are several ways which can help you to become mindful during the day. In this section of the chapter, we are going to cover a simple step-by-step process that you use to practice mindfulness.

Dedicate space and time

When choosing an area that you can use to practice your mindfulness, it's essential to settle for space which is not only calm but also one that is soothing and quiet. You also might want to pick up a time that you will less likely to be interrupted by your colleagues or family members.

Create a space within your home which is peaceful and also one that will allow you to calm down while immersed in your mindfulness practice.

It's essential to ensure that you only use this space for mindfulness alone and not for anything else. By doing this, when you decide to sit down, the body is going to be alerted that it's high time to cool down and then practice mindfulness.

Make an effort to be in the present without judgment

If you take a moment and then think about, the moment that you are indeed able to live will always be the present. Do not think about the past or the future; you have to acknowledge that you are in the present moment entirely. You can always go back to listening to the sounds that are in your surrounding and also focus on your breathing.

Do nothing and be yourself.

To get things accomplished, you do not necessarily have to be running around. Many at times our body and mind will always need to be recharged, so that when you can still become productive when you have some work to do. Always allow your body and mind to experience this quiescent period and then think of this period as an integral part of a healthy and fulfilling life.

Avoid thinking about the past or planning about the future.

We all know that we cannot change our pasts. Therefore, why can't we just let the past go? Take a moment and think of the things that transpired. Moreover, the future has hitherto come, and thus it serves us no purpose to focus intently in the future. In due time the future will come. Instead of worrying about the future or the past, you should instead focus on the present moment. Avoid worrying about the time that you are going to allow to waste before waking up.

Contemplate on words, motivations, thought, and actions.
When saying, thinking or undertaking an action, what's usually the motive behind the action? Are you telling a narrative to be beneficial to someone in one way or another, or are you just saying the story to be of benefit to your ego? Always take a moment and think about your real motivation behind a specific action. Try and find out whether it's necessary or not. Ensure that you are continuously coming from a high place when you decide to act or speak in a certain way.

Notice the judgment and these judgments pass

It's normal to have judgments. It's a healthy and natural thing that everyone gets to experience. Nonetheless, it is also imperative to recognize your thoughts and then allow these deliberations to pass without necessarily affecting your thoughts. Judgments usually are not permanent, and thus your mind can always change. Therefore, we should genuinely avoid getting caught up in our initial observations.

Return to the moment

If somehow you begin to get concerned about the impending future or start regretting about the past, then you can always return your attention to the present. Take a moment and recognize that there is nothing that you can be able to do or alter what has already happened. Alternatively, there are times when we cannot be able to change anything that will happen in the future. Therefore, you should always return to the here and now and live a peaceful life. Avoid being so tough on yourself, especially when your concentration drifts off. Always bring your attention to the present moment.

Every person's mind will wander from time to time, especially while in mindfulness meditation. It is always okay to acknowledge the passing thoughts and then let them go. Once these thoughts have gone, you should now take your time and then reorganize your focus to the mindfulness meditation. This is one of many mindfulness blueprints. As mentioned earlier, there are several ways that you can employ to practice mindfulness. Continue reading on, as we have included additional ways that you can use to apply mindfulness into your body.

Think about your true intentions

This does not necessarily have to be a time-consuming process. You can begin by identifying your primary reasons for partaking in mindfulness as well as your intended objectives. You might be looking for a way that you can be animated throughout, or you might just be aiming at reducing the judgment levels that you place on yourself while thinking every day.

Focus on your breath

Take a moment and contemplate on your breathing. Visualize the air flowing into and out of the respirational system. Moreover, you should also think about the physical sensations that you will be experiencing when breathing in and out as well as the falling and rising of your stomach and chest.

Always notice each time your mind begins to wander
Your account will walk from time to time, and thus, you should not try and force any thoughts to pass away. Whenever you see your mind wandering, then you can always return to your inhalation.

Always forgive the wandering mind

If the mind continues to wander forever, then you should avoid trying to fight the mind too much. Instead of wrestling with these thoughts, you should take a moment and observe these thoughts. You should practice not to react, as well. Continue sitting down and pay close attention. While it might be problematic to continue with your contemplation/meditation, technically there is nothing that else which you can be able to do. Instead, you should keep referring back to your breath.

Upon finishing the meditation, you should lift your gaze slowly There is isn't any wrong or right amount for reflection. However, if you are starting meditation, then you might want to first begin with the shorter sessions that are going to last for a maximum of 10 minutes. Once you start getting comfortable with your meditation, then you can start to practice for more extended periods.

Bring your attention slowly to your surrounding and the present You should recognize the space that's around you. You can begin to wiggle your toes and fingers slowly. You will then proceed to move the rest of the body and hands. Always take your time while getting up.
Moreover, you should also take your time and later notice any sound, music, or noise that's within your surrounding environment. Think about how your body truly feels from bottom to top. Also, think about the emotions and feelings.

Conclusion

Thank you for making it to the end of this book, Braining Training; Improving Your Cognitive Functions. We believe that you found the book quite informative and resourceful. Since you have completed this book, it's now time to begin your journey.

If you downloaded this book to know the basics of brain training then well and good. Conversely, if you downloaded this book to not only understand more about brain training but also improve your cognitive functions, then it's essential to try and recall everything valuable that you learned in the book.

We have provided well-researched data as well as scientific studies which show which of these methods you should follow and which you should overlook. While some brain training games are quite useful, many of them are just created for commercial purposes. Therefore, we highly advise you to screen each brain training program before adopting them.

Instead, if you are looking for ways to improve your cognitive skills, then we highly recommend cognitive-behavioral techniques such as mindfulness which is quite useful. We also highly encourage other CBT tools because just like mindfulness, science has shown that these techniques give tremendous results.

While we wait for such techniques to be introduced into clinical science, we highly recommend them to our readers instead of computer-based programs. CBT techniques can change our thought and patterns, and this is what makes these programs extremely useful.

by the same author

- **MINDSET OF SUCCESS**
  How to improve the potential of your mind and know what successful people think about business, psychology of success, relationships and life.
  ©2019

  (*Stephen Habits*)

- **SOCIAL SKILLS**
  Learn how to improve your speaking skills and empathic listening, simple persuasion strategies to improve conversation and influence people with your charisma.
  ©2019

  (*Stephen Habits*)

- **COGNITIVE BEHAVIORAL THERAPY**
  Change your life right now with simple techniques to manage and retrain your brain from anxiety and depression, learn how to fight panic, negative thinking and anger.
  ©2019

  (*Stephen Habits*)

www.ingramcontent.com/pod-product-compliance
Lightning Source LLC
Chambersburg PA
CBHW061802250726
48657CB00001B/249